COULD GOD BE THIS GOOD?

THE BEST NEWS YOU HAVE EVER HEARD IN YOUR LIFE

DR. M. TYRONE CUSHMAN

WESTBOW·
PRESS
A DIVISION OF THOMAS NELSON
& ZONDERVAN

WestBow Press books may be ordered through booksellers or by contacting:

WestBow Press
A Division of Thomas Nelson & Zondervan
1663 Liberty Drive
Bloomington, IN 47403
www.westbowpress.com
1 (866) 928-1240

ISBN: 978-1-4908-3326-2 (sc)
ISBN: 978-1-4908-3328-6 (hc)
ISBN: 978-1-4908-3327-9 (e)

Library of Congress Control Number: 2014906344

Printed in the United States of America.

WestBow Press rev. date: 08/26/2014

CONTENTS

IN MEMORY
Of

Jacqueline Ann Thomas-Cushman
1946 - 2013

I dedicate this book to the memory of "Jackie" my wife of 45 blessed years who went home Monday, August 12, 2013 at 1:25pm; who urged me to write and finish this book; who promised me distressed souls in the church and out were waiting for it; who, while sitting up in bed at night, would ask me to read to her the developing chapters and who patiently listened to me ramble on and on about what I thought God was saying then responding, "Oh Baby, write that down right now."

ACKNOWLEDGEMENTS

To Michael My Son and Namesake – who was my official screener; whose brilliant mind and generational perspective engaged me, challenged me, questioned me, debated me and who when I doubted myself affirmed me and pushed me forward.

To Sherita M. James, our adopted daughter, who passed away suddenly in 2004; who endured my impassioned explanations about the love of God; who even took notes of my spontaneous inspirations and who longed to see the finished product.

To Dr. Glovioell C. Rowland PhD., my gift from God; my former Executive Assistant, my mentor, my confidant and counselor; who in 1994 gave me many pep talks, an occasional rebuke, invaluable advice and to insure I would capture my spontaneous inspiration, the miniature cassette recorder which recorded my first thoughts; who elicited a promise that I would not die with this book inside of me; the woman of God who prayed me through some difficult days.

To The Pasadena Church of God now the Pasadena Church – who from 1979 to 2000 evolved with a young Pastor as a loyal, loving community influencing people of every walk of life for the sake of God's Kingdom; who tolerated my doctrinal extremes and grew with me to the more moderate and livable place of faith we hold today.

To "Zion's Hill" - West Middlesex, PA – where I grew up; where I served; where I learned hard lessons; where I fell in love with the church, "the Saints," and "the songs of Zion"; where I raised my family and spent some of the best years of my life – "Oh Church of God - I love thy courts."

DEDICATION

This book is dedicated to the un-churched and the non-believer; to those who believe that they have done too much and messed up too bad and too often to ever be included in God's love; to those who have been hurt by the church, religious people and the drama and trauma of family history; to Believers who are tired of fighting other Believers and finally to those Believers who want to be ambassadors of God's love, grace and mercy...ONLY.

PROLOGUE

Could God Be This Good – The Goal

- To assure the Believer and Non-believer of God's unconditional love.
- To equip the Body with "Good News Talking Points" about God's determination and strategy to save.
- To teach the message and ministry of reconciliation
- To inspire everyday Believers to become true global ambassadors in the spirit of 2 Corinthians 5:16-21.
- To teach the universal simplicity of *God's* gospel - salvation by grace through faith
- To teach that His grace and faith are wide and accessible to all people everywhere.
- To give who ever needs it fresh hope and assurance as we hit life's turbulence just before landing.

The Big-Tent God

It may be helpful to know the mind-set of the author as you read. Know first that I have been very careful to use the Bible as my rule of faith and primary reference. It follows that my facts and even my opinions, though subject to interpretation, are Christocentric; in other words, from a Christian perspective.

I have shared what I believe to be revelation on the size of God and how that view impacts our religious worldview. My primary premise is that God did not create a broad heterogeneous range of people of different colors, cultures, and histories and then limit His choice for those who will receive His eternal favor to a narrow homogenous sliver of humanity. Our God, Jehovah-Elohim, is the God of the big tent. By *big tent* I mean He is one who by His very nature is inclusive of those who have practices, beliefs, or names for Him that differ from mine.

God Is Jesus, Jesus Is God

I have intentionally interchanged the use of the names *God* and *Jesus*. For example, *the blood of God* or *when God died on the cross* are statements attempting to express that though I believe in one God with three manifestations—God the Father, God the Son, and God the Holy Spirit—it is the one God I am talking about. This may be one of the most important themes in the book. Since Jesus is God in the flesh, human beings may subconsciously diminish the person of Jesus and inadvertently diminish His purpose, His work, and His power to save because of his fleshly likeness. "*God* was reconciling the world to Himself in Christ, not counting men's sins against them" (2 Cor. 5:19, emphasis added) is one of the most powerful scriptures in the Holy Bible. When people understand it was God in the flesh who saved them, it changes the dynamic and the superlative from *great* to *greatest of all possible Saviors*. Absolutely nothing trumps God. Neither Satan nor sin, nor religion, nor race, nor culture, nor nationality, nor family mess can defeat God and, more importantly, His plan to save us all.

Repetition and Terms

In order to drive home certain points, I have used certain Bible passages repeatedly. For purposes of clarity or emphasis, I have sometimes used different Bible translations for the same scriptural passage. Like viewing the various facets of a diamond, I use these various translations then intentionally return to the key themes regarding the goodness of God over and over. When I use the term – "He has saved us all" I mean it figuratively; I do NOT mean it in a literal sense. I believe some, not most, will be lost. Likewise, when I say "God wins" I mean it literally. I believe God and good win over Satan and evil however you keep score.

Religion versus Relationship

A formal definition of *religion*, according to *Encarta World English Dictionary,* is "beliefs and opinions concerning the existence, nature and worship of a deity; a particular system of beliefs and practices relating to the divine." Though the formal definition is adequate for most purposes, I have chosen to use the term *religion* in most places in this book to contrast with the idea of *relationship* with God. Religion, for the purposes of this book, refers to the secular opinions and rituals about God as opposed to a personal relationship with Him. *Religion* is not intended as a negative term; *religion* is, however, in the author's view, of lesser value than relationship.

I invite you to explore with me the wonders and the magnitude of God's love for every human being in the world. He saves, heals, protects, provides, and delivers all who seek Him however they seek Him. Because He loves us, in time, God mitigates every tragedy and forgives every sin that takes place. By the curing and covering blood of Jesus, He brings us back home to an afterlife in eternity with Him. After reading this book, may you rejoice with me as we wonder together, *could God be this good?*

To Whom It May "Concern"

This book, *Could God Be This Good* does NOT intentionally represent a particular theology or doctrine. This book is what its title suggests – an inspired Word-based speculation about the extent of Gods' love, grace and goodness. My interpretation of Scripture is therefore influenced by my anticipation of Gods' super-hero qualities and His absolute sovereignty. That means - He has the power, ability and authority to do anything He wants to do my human understanding… notwithstanding.

Hence, my conclusions and logic attempts to draw upon the patterns of God in scripture that are universal. You might call them universal standards. Such patterns and standards are easily seen, universally applicable and covers all possible conditions and variables. For example, the facts may not always apply everywhere the same but the truth does. A practice may be national but a principle is universal. 2 Corinthians 3:6b says:"…the letter killeth but the spirit gives life." God's truth is always universal and inclusive of all variables. Salvation and/or the gospel, therefore, must be accessible and applicable to all humankind everywhere under all conditions. If it cannot be universally applied, it is perhaps lawful but not expedient and therefore not intended by God as a "living principle." Truth must pass the test of universal application.

Consequently, I do not claim to be theologically or politically, perfectly correct seeing as how perfect correctness depends upon whose theology, among the many, my words are being measured by.

Should you need to, I give you the permission to reduce my words to a philosophy in order to preserve our relationship, your denomination's interpretations and the unique spins you place on the scriptures that I use in my "speculative" conclusions.

An example of my "principle trumps practice" or the spirit of a thing supercedes the letter of that thing is: I caught my daughter Carmen stealing cookies at the tender age of three. If she had suddenly died, my training taught me she would go to hell for eternity; that is forever and ever and ever - and that, for me, was unbelievable. Carmen knew the Lord's Prayer; she loved to sing and throw both hands in the air in praise and could tell you that she loved Jesus. But, she was a thief. Instinctively, I knew there was something greater than her sin but my church background had only prepared me for the worst. I was never taught the love of God to that degree. I was convinced that the Sovereign God *could* condemn her to hell; I just could not bring myself to believe that God *would*.

What this means is that either I do not believe in the hell that I say I believe is clearly taught in the Bible or I believe that God has a plan of redemption for willful unrepentant cookie thieves who don't get the chance or don't know they have to repent. This book helps us discover the latter. Life and scripture teaches God is that good and that reasonable.

Why is this important? It is important because it enables us to be the ambassadors of 2 Corinthians 5:20 and to be the bearers of the Good News of Jesus Christ to everybody everywhere in all conditions. Believers can bear witness to the power of the Gospel without having to memorize human theologies and denominational catechisms. God is sovereign. His blood is sovereignly applied. His grace, mercy and love are Sovereign gifts.

It is my sincere hope that most of you who read this book will agree that it is the best news you have ever heard in your life. However, I realize that Good News is often the victim of unbelief and misinterpretation. So I am sure that some of you will not be able to receive the news that God is greater than The Evil One; grace wins over sin; Jesus' death and resurrection defeated death, hell and the grave and that the supreme love and goodness of the Sovereign Almighty Jehovah leads humankind to faith, repentance and back home to Him. You may not be able to believe that God will find you and love you wherever you are in the world and most of you, through a faith He will gift to you, will acknowledge Him and instantly be covered by His divine already shed blood from that moment forward. Sadly, a relative few will choose not to acknowledge Him even when He is revealed to them and suffer the consequences.

This book is intended to be a revelation and a rationale for God's divine strategy of love. While I do not believe the extremes of the so called doctrines of Universalism and Inclusion, any likeness is without apology, coincidental and no less true because of the association. Truth is true no matter who says it. I believe that God so loved the world He saved it - period - our religious labels and limited intelligence, interpretations and even wild charges of heresy notwithstanding. Should you conclude that God is not as good as I suggest, just know that I love you without condition and so does God.

A Personal Note

I write this book driven by an inside knowledge of the private struggles of Believers to maintain their faith. I know powerful men of God AND many Christian Believers who had/have besetting sins; sins they denounced, repented for, wept over yet seemed never to be completely delivered from. They could preach the hide off the devil, lay hands on the sick and the sick recovered, bind and cast out demons then fall on their faces and scream "O God who shall deliver *me* from *mine*?"

Some of these men of God and many, many everyday people died in faith believing that the grace, mercy and goodness of God would follow them to their graves and on into eternity and that they would dwell in the house of The Lord - Home - forever and ever.

Some of those men and women are reading this book and screaming out in their souls for deliverance, peace and explanation. I sought God's face for rationale and understanding of how God saves distressed souls who have besetting sins that stalk them through life and all the way to their graves.

Well, I have a message from The Lord. He says to tell you He's got you, stay in Him because "there is no condemnation to those who are in Christ Jesus, who walk not after the flesh but who walk after the Spirit...". I write to you to tell you that God is greater than your sin and where your sins did abound His grace did much more abound and that you are saved and no matter what it looks like you will be saved because Almighty God has died to save you. He warns you that there are real-time consequences for sin; that your deliverance will come as you become a slave to right living. God is looking at you through blood-shaded lens. He sees you in the future and you look a whole lot better than you do right now. Keep walking!

Peace.

Preface

An Apology

On behalf of the church in general and the Christian church in particular, and on behalf of every prelate, whether apostle, bishop, cardinal, pastor, priest, nun, preacher, reverend, imam, monk, rinpoche, lama, or any other religious leader who, in the name of God, has intentionally or unintentionally misrepresented the simplicity of God's gospel and kingdom, I apologize.

I realize it is an audacious presumption to think that I could represent, not to mention speak for, other religious organizations and their ministers, but it seems to me that we, the professional clergy of the world, owe the people of the world, whom the sovereign Jehovah said He would save, an apology for all the confusion, division, denominationalism, sectarianism, territorialism, fear-mongering, narcissism, exploitation, politics, power grabs, immorality, and abuse some of us have perpetrated upon them in His holy name over millennia.

Please forgive our humanity that even during the best of times sometimes breaks through and exposes our personal agendas, our private interpretations, our religious fears and our secret sins. In spite of what we may presumptuously decree and declare, in spite of our regal robes, royal titles, and high seats, we confess we are not God. We are flesh and blood. Many of us are called, a few of us are chosen, and some of us—though not all who have gone—are sent.

We humbly acknowledge that when we are doing our jobs well, we are representatives of His love, His peace, His grace, His mercy, His righteousness, and His joy—nothing more, nothing less, and nothing else.

INTRODUCTION

My mother was the kindest, most patient woman I have ever known. She prayed unceasingly, and to her seven children, she was a saint. Her wisdom was recognized and celebrated throughout the Eight Mile Road housing projects where my siblings and I were born, and then up and down Anglin Street in Detroit, Michigan, where we were raised. People from all walks of life came to our house, seeking my mother's advice and the laying on of her loving hands in prayer for healing and deliverance from all kinds of bondage, both real and imagined. She took to her grave the secrets of many men and women, from prominent to everyday people.

One bright summer day when I was eleven years old, I burst into the kitchen as she was preparing dinner to ask her some serious questions, questions so serious they kept me awake at night. "Mama, if a baby dies before it's old enough to hear about Jesus, will it go to heaven?" I asked. Before she could answer, I asked my follow-up question: "And will the people in the darkest part of Africa who have never heard of Jesus be lost and go to hell?"

She gave me her classic first response: "What do you think?"

I answered with typical preadolescent sacrilege. "Well, I don't think it would be fair if people who didn't ask to be born in the first place and then didn't hear about Jesus and didn't know any better would go to hell. And I think God is fair," I added.

She didn't just look at me; she stared as if to say, *Where did all that come from?* I had her full attention. In a low, raspy alto, as if to say, *This is off the record,* she spoke softly. "Well, I also think He's fair; and even more than being fair, I think He is so wise and loving that He has figured that out already. That's why He needs you to grow up and carry the gospel as far and as wide as you can. I am sure He will do the rest." Before she returned to stirring the cornbread batter, she added, "His hand is on you, baby. Mama's praying for you."

I remember walking away thinking, *But that's not what they said in Sunday school.*

Nonetheless, in spite of my Sunday school lessons, Bible college theology, university training, forty-plus years as a pastor, and five years as general overseer of my denomination, my mother's wisdom has outlasted all the rigid orthodoxies of my beloved Holiness tradition. As I travel around the world, I am fascinated by the many wonderful manifestations of God, goodwill, and genuine human kindness practiced by believers of many different religious stripes who love God with all their heart, mind, body, and soul.

This book is about God's marvelous grace and power to save us all. If you are a novice, one who has not been a Christian for long or raised in church, then what you are about to read will help you instantly. You will be encouraged and empowered to witness with great joy and confidence, and perhaps with fewer inhibitions.

If you are a veteran believer and a member of a religious sect or denomination or a member of an independent denomination and have been indoctrinated with the tenets of your faith since childhood, you will be challenged. Nonetheless, I think you will really enjoy this quick, easy, and provocative read about the simplicity and the goodness of God. It may relax you from the unintentional consequence of religious stress, competition and confusion.

If you harbor quiet suspicions and nagging doubts about your religion or religion in general, this book may be a game changer.

Regardless of the category you fall in, you will swallow hard on some things and raise your eyebrows on others, but I promise you will come away convinced that God is good—so good, in fact, you will rethink your approach to evangelism, suspend at least some of your certainty of judgment of others, and believe more in the kingdom of God, or His universal church, than your religious denomination ever taught you.

CHAPTER 1

CAN'T SEE THE FOREST FOR LOOKING AT THE TREES

Jesus did many other things as well. If every one of them
were written down, I suppose that even the whole world
would not have room for the books that would be written
—JOHN 21:25 (NIV)

As a young man, I was always depressed by the thought that so many people were going to spend eternity in hell unless I could reach them with the gospel of Jesus Christ... and lead them into receiving baptism by submersion in water... and bring them into the baptism in the Holy Ghost... and then persuade them to attend a church called by the only name in the New Testament given for a church, the "Church of God,"... then have them become part of the reformation movement of the Church of God because it was God's "last reformation"... and show them how to walk in holiness of lifestyle... and teach them how to practice the gifts of the Spirit—well, at least some of the gifts (even though some of us think we practice all of them)... etc., etc., etc. I think you get the picture.

Deep inside I knew God had not left the world that He—the all-powerful, all-knowing, present-everywhere-at-the-same-time God—died for in the hands of well-meaning though often confused Christian believers. So I did what most who have been on this Christian journey for any appreciable length of time eventually do. First, I gradually moderated my view and understanding of the Word of God and began to leave room for mystery. Second, I accepted the fact that God was bigger than my church background (after all, the Church of God was only two hundred thousand strong). Third—and this began my breakthrough—I concluded that truth was not relative, but context was, and that God was probably more generous, accepting, and inclusive than I had been taught.

The Mystery That Is God

It is now fifty-seven years later and far from Mama's kitchen-table wisdom. At the delightful age of sixty-eight, I have discovered the older I get, the less I know. I actually have more questions now than I have answers. I don't get it. When I was sixteen, I knew everything. Now that's what I call some serious regression!

The truth is, age allows one to accumulate, sort and prioritize information. It allows one to pray for understanding, then summarize and draw conclusions. I have just reached the age where I am able to draw a few conclusions about how good God is. My observations are open-ended, which means I have not closed the book. I still struggle to keep an open mind. I'm still filled with wide-eyed wonder and a hunger to know more. I've changed my mind about some things more than once. I'm still learning. I'm amazed at an unfolding discovery of God's infinite love and kindness. In the realm of time, I'm what they call a "senior citizen." But in God's eternal presence, I always feel like a child.

The phenomenon of moderating one's views must be a function of age. To my amazement, greater men than I have come to similar conclusions and have adjusted their personal end-of-life views to reflect a much broader and inclusive theology. For instance, famed author and expositor William Barclay, as he neared the end of his life, came to the conclusion that in the end all would be saved. He rejected what he had taught his entire life: that many would find themselves in eternal torment in a place called hell. Near the end of his life, William Barclay, famous for many writings but especially for his commentaries of the Old and New Testaments that so many preachers and scholars quote, believed in universal salvation. In his autobiography, he states: "But in one thing, I would go beyond strict orthodoxy—I am a convinced universalist. I believe that in the end all men will be gathered into the love of God (William Barclay, *A Spiritual Autobiography*, William B. Eerdmans Publishing Co., 1975, p. 65).

As dramatic—and for some, traumatic—as William Barclay's confession is, the real mind-blower for me was the interview Billy Graham gave to the noted journalist Jon Meacham of *Newsweek* magazine. One could call it an amazing end of life confession as Dr. Graham seems to soften his traditional view of his "core message" and declares God's love for all people of the world as God's "priority." The interview not only exposed Dr. Graham's late in life belief that the Bible is open for interpretation, which is a tremendous statement in itself, but when asked if he believed heaven will include Jews, Muslims, Buddhists, Hindus or secular people Graham joins the ranks of the so-called theological "inclusionist" when he says,

> Those are decisions only the Lord will make. I believe
> the love of God is absolute. He said He gave His son

for the whole world and I think He loves everybody
regardless of what label they have. (Jon Meacham,
Newsweek, Billy Graham In Twilight; August 14,
2006; page 43).

That final quote of Billy Graham stood me straight up. I was
infused with a sudden dose of courage for my own emerging point
of view. I humbly concurred with one of the greatest Christians of
our time: "I spend more time on the love of God than I used to…
I believe the love of God is absolute… I think he loves everybody
regardless of what label they have." Billy Graham, in my mind,
has long been the greatest evangelist of our time. As the sun sets
on his life, the statement he made to the *Newsweek* interviewer
should instruct us all in the breadth, depth, and width of God's
love. We serve a good God and a big God.

As a child, my wonder about the bigness of God sent my mind
spinning and drew me into endless possibilities and implications.
How big was God? This was at once both fascinating and
frustrating, and it remains so even today.

It is fascinating because of the sheer magnitude of His being.
He is ageless; He has no beginning and no ending; He always
was and always will be; He is without peer; He made everything
that is; He is all-powerful; He is unlimited; He is everywhere
at once; He is all-knowing and all-sufficient. He shares these
characteristics with no one. As His Word says, "That they may
know from the rising of the sun, and from the west, that there
is none beside me. I am the LORD, and there is none else. I form
the light, and create darkness: I make peace, and create evil: I the
LORD do all these things" (Isaiah. 45:6–7 KJV). No good exists
that does not come from Him, and no evil exists that He did not
cause to form.

It is frustrating because of my human limitations of intelligence
and understanding. No matter how hard I try, I can't wrap my

mind around the complex genius of the Godhead, the concept of time and eternity, the physics of the universe, and the spiritual connection we have with the Creator of it all. It is frustrating, intimidating, and fascinating all at once because it is the finite trying to understand the infinite. It is like trying to wrap one's arms around a circle... from the inside.

Consequently, when I read in the Holy Bible, and specifically in the last verse in John's gospel, "And there are also many other things which Jesus did, the which, if they should be written every one, I suppose that even the world itself could not contain the books that should be written" (John 21:25 KJV), I am unable to accept that any man or woman or any group of men, women, scholars, philosophers, modern-day preachers, prophets, or pundits have an exclusive corner on understanding the eternal relationship between God and man. At best, when we put them all together, we can arrive at reasonable principles that help guide us home to Him.

This book, therefore, represents my attempt and my exhortation to others to step back from the trees in order to see the forest. I believe we human beings were built to win. I believe we were fashioned in eternity, complete with built-in corrections for the flaws that would develop in the time realm because of the free radical of free will.

I believe, therefore, that the flaws and sins of humankind have been accounted for and provided for from before the foundation of the world. All sins and their consequences—from serial murder to self-murder; from heinous tortures, rapes, racism, and wars to; all diseases and every sickness, whether physical, mental, or religious—were laid on Jesus and borne away. The most important phrases Jesus uttered from the cross were "Father, forgive them," and "It is finished." He spoke those words, as He died the most horrible, unfair, and undeserved death any man could suffer. He was holy, just, and good. He died for us—the unholy, the unjust, and the un-good. Yet He said, "Father, forgive them." I'll say more about that later.

Through the messianic prophet Isaiah, God made this stunning and prophetic declaration of commitment to us all:

Who believes what we've heard and seen?
Who would have thought GOD's saving power would look like this?
The servant grew up before God—a scrawny seedling,
a scrubby plant in a parched field.
There was nothing attractive about him,
nothing to cause us to take a second look.
He was looked down on and passed over,
a man who suffered, who knew pain firsthand.
One look at him and people turned away.
We looked down on him, thought he was scum.
But the fact is, it was *our* pains he carried—
our disfigurements, all the things wrong with *us*.
We thought he brought it on himself,
that God was punishing him for his own failures.
But it was our sins that did that to him,
that ripped and tore and crushed him—*our sins!*
He took the punishment, and that made us whole.
Through his bruises we get healed.
We're all like sheep who've wandered off and gotten lost.
We've all done our own thing, gone our own way.
And GOD has piled all our sins, everything we've done wrong,
on him, on him.
He was beaten, he was tortured,
but he didn't say a word.
Like a lamb taken to be slaughtered
and like a sheep being sheared,

he took it all in silence.
Justice miscarried, and he was led off—
and did anyone really know what was happening?
He died without a thought for his own welfare,
beaten bloody for the sins of my people.
They buried him with the wicked,
threw him in a grave with a rich man,
Even though he'd never hurt a soul
or said one word that wasn't true.
Still, it's what GOD had in mind all along,
to crush him with pain.
The plan was that he give himself as an offering for sin
so that he'd see life come from it—life, life, and more
life.
And GOD's plan will deeply prosper through him.
Out of that terrible travail of soul,
he'll see that it's worth it and be glad he did it.
Through what he experienced, my righteous one, my
servant,
will make many "righteous ones,"
as he himself carries the burden of their sins.
Therefore I'll reward him extravagantly—
the best of everything, the highest honors—
Because he looked death in the face and didn't flinch,
because he embraced the company of the lowest.
He took on his own shoulders the sin of the many,
he took up the cause of all the black sheep.

—ISAIAH 53:1–12 (MSG)

In this passage, the prophet Isaiah describes God's premeditation and execution of His comprehensive plan for the offering of the perfect sacrifice. It is not only a rationale, but also a preview of the salvation of humankind and the ultimate victory of good over evil.

Truth over Theology

By no means is this book intended to be a conclusive theological or doctrinal finding, though it does press for a real-world understanding of the Isaiah passage above. I am not writing as the advocate or adversary of any particular theology. I am attempting to step back from the trees in order to see the forest. The plan of salvation is comprehensive and inclusive of every variable, all diversity, and the entire spectrum of good and evil experiences. That is precisely why it requires the all-wise and all-knowing God of eternity and time to premeditate the plan accordingly.

Could God Be This Good? is a studied opinion, a logical line of thought based on the Word and ongoing revelation. It could be themed "things that make us go *hmmm.*" So don't take this book or yourself so seriously that you consign me or my musings to hell for what your tradition and denomination might call heresy.

I hope these pages will delight and assure those of you who doubt. I pray that what you read will expand your faith while exalting the goodness of God and giving you good-news talking points to share with everyday people. My words are an attempt to discover and praise His eternal wisdom and awesome power to save. Every time I think I have found a line of limitation in God, He says something in His Word or does something in my life that crosses the line. I have not yet discovered the limits of His love and goodness, and if the truth be told, I'm no longer looking. I am only asking, could God be as good as His Word implies?

I understand that some of us feel safer living with limits. Ironically, we tend to fight to believe the worst. The subconscious and ever-present sin nature constantly competes with the Creator for the center or for earned credits that give us a role and a right to be saved. No wonder God has said "not of works, lest any man should boast" (Eph. 2:10 KJV). We instinctively believe the harder a thing is, the better it is. If it's tight, it's right.

I choose to believe that when Jesus said, "It is finished," God in Christ locked down the victory over all sin for all time and for all humankind. When my private concepts of God finally gave way to the revelation of His limitless, sovereign love, I was freed to love Him, and now I rejoice in the endeavor to keep His commandments.

Verse 1 of my all-time favorite song, "The Love of God," by Frederick M. Lehman says it well:

> The love of God is greater far
> Than tongue or pen can ever tell;
> It goes beyond the highest star,
> And reaches to the lowest hell;
> The guilty pair, bowed down with care,
> God gave His Son to win;
> His erring child He reconciled,
> And pardoned from his sin.

CHAPTER 2

THE GOD OF REASON

Come. Sit down. Let's argue this out. This is GOD's Message: If your sins are blood-red, they'll be snow-white. If they're red like crimson, they'll be like wool.

—ISAIAH 1:18 MSG

I believe whatever God wills happens eventually in principle or in practice:

> In the beginning of God's preparing the heavens and the earth—the earth hath existed waste and void, and darkness [is] on the face of the deep, and the Spirit of God fluttering on the face of the waters, and God saith, "Let light be"; and light is.
>
> —GENESIS 1:1–3 YLT

I believe that eternity and time line up behind the will of God. I believe that time and all of its variables have been perfectly planned in eternity by God. I believe that nothing exists in either eternity or in time that has not been created by God.

> For through him God created everything in heaven
> and on earth, the seen and the unseen things, including
> spiritual powers, lords, rulers, and authorities. God
> created the whole universe through him and for him.
> Christ existed before all things, and in union with
> him all things have their proper place.
>
> —COLOSSIANS 1:16–17 GNT

I believe that when God decided to save the world, He saved it notwithstanding its cultures, races, languages, customs, traditions, or inevitable religions.

> For God so loved the world that he gave his one and
> only Son, that whoever believes in him shall not perish
> but have eternal life.
>
> —JOHN 3:16

To save a condemned world wallowing in chaos and confusion, He came down to that world wrapped in human flesh and paid its penalty—past, present, and future. I believe that the *death* of the omnipotent, omniscient God (Jesus) trumps and transcends everything in time from beginning to end. I believe that when God died on the cross as Jesus, He was not making a sudden move of desperation. He was acting according to plan and died for all sin in every form, whether it be the sin of people or the sin of religions.

> Yet the rescuing gift is not exactly parallel to the death-
> dealing sin. If one man's sin put crowds of people
> at the dead-end abyss of separation from God, just
> think what God's gift poured through one man, Jesus
> Christ, will do! There's no comparison between that
> death-dealing sin and this generous, life-giving gift.
> The verdict on that one sin was the death sentence;

the verdict on the many sins that followed was this
wonderful life sentence. If death got the upper hand
through one man's wrongdoing, can you imagine
the breathtaking recovery life makes, sovereign life,
in those who grasp with both hands this wildly
extravagant life-gift, this grand setting-everything-
right, that the one man Jesus Christ provides?
—ROMANS 5:15–17 MSG

Going to heaven is not a function of right religion, but a
function of reconciled relationship.

But the basic reality of God is plain enough. Open
your eyes and there it is! By taking a long and
thoughtful look at what God has created, people have
always been able to see what their eyes as such can't
see: eternal power, for instance, and the mystery of
his divine being. So nobody has a good excuse. What
happened was this: People knew God perfectly well,
but when they didn't treat him like God, refusing to
worship him, they trivialized themselves into silliness
and confusion so that there was neither sense nor
direction left in their lives. They pretended to know
it all, but were illiterate regarding life. They traded the
glory of God who holds the whole world in his hands
for cheap figurines you can buy at any roadside stand.

—ROMANS 1:19–23 MSG

God the Father clothed His Word in human flesh that came
down from heaven to earth in the form of the Son of God, Jesus
Christ. He died on the cross for the sins of the world, and then He
rose from the dead and ascended into heaven. He came back as
promised in the form of the Holy Spirit to give us power over sin,
Satan, and self. He gave us all the ability to know Him, to become

His sons and daughters, to join Him in the establishment of His kingdom on the earth, which the Holy Bible calls the "kingdom of God." Our task is to spread the Good News of the kingdom, the message of reconciliation, as found in 2 Corinthians 5:19. That message paraphrased says, "Come on home. Daddy is not mad at you. He has paid your penalty forward."

I also believe that each of us walks out our reconciled relationship with God in direct proportion to our revelation of Him. And that is determined only by God Himself, who factors in variables of context, opportunity, background, and the breadth and depth of His love, grace, and mercy.

I truly believe that the many different religions stem from man's instinctive response to God's powerful and eternal imprinted image on all humankind. I believe that those religions notwithstanding, Jesus Christ is God's only Savior and that His death and resurrection reduce all other religions and religious leaders to imperfect cultural and religious icons who inadvertently create God in man's own image, but whose efforts to lead humankind to God are honored by God in the strong name of Jesus. I want to believe that Jehovah God tolerates and forgives the innocent religious orthodoxies that have evolved as a result of man's search for Him.

The late Dr. Horace W. Sheppard Sr., one of the great preachers of my lifetime, was famous for declaring himself "Catholic, because I believe the church is the universal body of Christ; Baptist, because I have been to the water; Church of God, because I believe the church belongs to God; Methodist, because I methodically study and try to adopt His method; Pentecostal, because I have been baptized in the Holy Ghost like on the day of Pentecost; Jehovah's Witness, because Jehovah is His name and I am one of His witnesses." Of course, by the time he finished his recitation, he had covered every denomination he could think of, and the members of his audience were on their feet, shouting back with great joy and affirmation.

Now, each of those denominations is Christian. But some of us Christians were raised to believe some of those other Christian denominations were satanic deceptions and their followers would go to hell. Well, it seems to me that error is error, whether it is Christian or non-Christian. So, if Dr. Sheppard is suggesting that the blood of Jesus covers the sin of error and misunderstanding, what prevents it from covering the ignorance and misunderstanding of a non-Christian "believer"? Hold on— keep reading!

Case in Point

I find it significant, wonderful, and prophetic that God made the same promise to Hagar as He did to Abraham, knowing that Hagar and her son, Ishmael, would become the progenitors of Islam. Though Ishmael was not the child of *the* promise, he was the child of *a* promise. Ishmael was, in fact, the first child of the covenant, but not the child of promise, thus indicating that God was prepared to handle this division of faith, knowing He would bring it together in Christ at Calvary. More about that later...

It seems so difficult for humankind to keep the revelation of God as simple, believable, and accessible as God left it. God accepts those who acknowledge Him by whatever means available, and He likewise rejects those who refuse to acknowledge Him even though He has revealed Himself to them. Additionally, to whom much is given, much is required. In other words, some of us are blessed with greater revelation than others, and we are therefore in a wonderful position to be greater ambassadors of that revelation.

The Danger of Orthodoxy

There is great danger in orthodoxy, not because of any one doctrinal or theological emphasis, but because of the potential and practice of exclusion that stems from it. The Greek word *orthodoxos,* from which we get the English word *orthodoxy,* literally means "of the right opinion." The question is, who determines the right opinion? That spirit of exclusion and division that orthodoxy can easily unintentionally promote has been spiritual kryptonite to the universal body of believers throughout the ages.

The development of common-sense faith in this high-tech, postmodern, ecumenical, relativistic, humanistic age is neither simple nor certain and probably requires some supernatural intervention. It is clear to me that our extremes evolve from sacred opinions that crystallize and solemnize into orthodoxies that are then rehearsed for millennia. These orthodoxies take on a history and life of their own, fixed doctrines developed from fixed theologies. Over time, they become the standard beliefs that form religious foundation and define the purist sect within any religious body. Their adherents are the "orthodox" believers, believers who tolerate little variance and no compromise, no matter what the evolution of revelatory truth should bring.

It is these tightly held orthodoxies that more often than not perpetuate toxic understandings and lead to deadly intolerance and damaging extremes that really do more harm than good. It is equally clear to me that religious orthodoxy has inadvertently aided and abetted religious extremism that ironically makes all religion unbelievable, even detestable. The resulting man-made religious divisions have enjoyed the cover of strong and enduring theological traditions that define their orthodoxies more than they define God. Competing religions use God to justify their imperialistic—though sometimes thought to be evangelistic—agendas.

The Game Changer

Jesus' birth heralded a new beginning for all peoples. He launched a new paradigm relative to race, gender, nationality, and religion. He broke with the strict orthodoxy of His Jewish religion and cut across the expectation of non-Jews. He disregarded religious protocols and set loose a nuclear chain reaction that launched the all-inclusive kingdom of God. His coming was the game changer.

Jesus' death and resurrection are the fulfillment of God's promise to Satan: "And I will put enmity between thee and the woman, and between thy seed and her seed; it shall bruise thy head, and thou shalt bruise his heel" (Gen. 3:15 KJV); and His covenant promise to Abraham: "All peoples on earth will be blessed through you" (Gen. 12:3). The problem is, we refuse to believe that *all* means "all." Could God be *that* good?

This fulfillment continued with Simeon's prophetic declaration, as recorded in Luke 2:30–32: "For my eyes have seen your salvation, which you have prepared in the sight of all people, a light for revelation to the Gentiles and for the glory to your people Israel." It culminated with great clarity when the apostle Peter confronted his racist and religious orthodoxy in a vision and was told, "Do not call anything impure that God has made clean" (Acts 10:15).

Following Peter's personal revelation, we see an even more powerful public revelation: "He [Peter] said to them: 'You are well aware that it is against our law for a Jew to associate with a Gentile or visit him.'… Then Peter began to speak: 'I now realize how true it is that God does not show favoritism' " (Acts 10:28,

34). This revelation united the Old and New Testament churches and established the new covenant precedent of multiracial and multinational unity in the kingdom of God.

The Bottom Line

I want everybody to go to heaven when they die. I do not begrudge anybody heaven. If Satan can somehow change from his created nature and purpose, good for him. Read my lips: *I don't care.* I also expect heaven to be a paradise where there is no sadness, sorrow, or sickness, and no memory of any pain, shame, dirt, or devil—a place where I'm finally safe forever from all hurt, harm, and danger. And while we're at it, I hope heaven has no religions, races, classes, or gender divisions. Now, that's what I call heaven!

Before you run to your liberal-versus-conservative theology corners, consider your motivation. Ask yourself whether it is the relentless pursuit of the truth (*aletheia,* the Greek word for *truth* that translates "unhiddenness") that drives you or the disparate desire to worship the traditionally held sacred cows of belief. Has the revelation of God ceased? Is it possible for any saged and sainted human theological understanding or misunderstanding, no matter how well intentioned, to undo what I call "the blood of God"—Jesus' death on the cross of Calvary? Can you un-ring the bell? Can any act of man undo Calvary?

While you're at it, ask yourself: *Why wouldn't I want everybody to go to heaven? Why should I care who gets in?* What's with this innate thing in us that insists on separation, segregation, and exclusion from those who are not like us or who don't believe what our group believes? Why do we spend one sickening second arguing over who's in and who's out? It is the blood of Jesus—not yours or anyone else's blood—that covers us all and gives us all safe passage home to heaven.

So, why wouldn't you want as many people as possible to be included in that awesome victory at the cross? Why would anyone cheer for an interpretation that promotes an exclusive few (or an exclusive many, for that matter)? When I see this human bent to instinctively exclude others based on religion, race, doctrine or any other reason, I am reminded that we are all, according to Scripture, born in sin and shaped in iniquity, so I should expect humanistic spin. And even as believers, we suffer from the side effects of being born and shaped in sin, and our perspectives are thus shaded by the side effects of sin.

Would you begrudge the thief on the cross his last-minute gift from the bleeding and dying Jesus who created him? Remember, the thief fits no theological model. He never confessed Jesus Christ as Lord and Savior. He was never baptized in water or in the Holy Ghost. To our knowledge, he was not even religious. He lived as a rogue and died as a confessed and convicted rogue who took a chance and acknowledged Jesus, a man he didn't know. He played the odds with nothing to lose. His last act in life was a shot in the dark, albeit his best. He embraced the possibility that Jesus would include him in His kingdom. I ask you, could God be this good to everybody everywhere?

What is the rationale? What are the pros and cons of the God who seems to be more inclusive than exclusive, who, according to John 3:16, died as the ultimate act of love for the world, not for the limiting religions of that world? I contend there must be a rationale that describes, defines, and summarizes the extent of how good God is. Divine revelation must intersect human reason at a point that makes the whole thing work if it is to be viable and credible among free-willing and free thinking humanity; otherwise, what is the point?

If God is the God of all, He must be explainable in all languages and in consideration of all the variables that we all were born into. Our answers must pass the test of universal relevance and applicability. Only then can the Holy Bible's claim of one sheepfold (John 10:16) make sense. And another thing, whatever the answer to this mystery of difference and the lack of homogeneity, it doesn't have to be understood by all groups. This eliminates the need for one group to define another. One experience does not fit all.

The intelligence of the men and women of God who represent Him as deputized oracles to a laity equally called by God as "ministers of reconciliation" and "living epistles" begs minimal vindication. At best, we represent God as His ambassadors. Our mission is to bear witness to His love and grace to every race, nationality, culture, time, and tongue.

Common sense compels us to keep the Good News, good news, even as we evolve in our understanding of Him. We acknowledge the evolution of truth, interpretation, understanding, and application. We also acknowledge satanic attempts to counteract, confuse, complicate, and co-opt the message of God's goodness. Deciphering doctrine and memorizing religious catechisms do not always speak of Good News to a troubled human being.

Again, I believe the goodness of the eternal God transcends time, language, culture, place, interpretation, and understanding of truth by those created in His image. I confess to you here and now, I don't know how He will do it, but I believe with all my heart that in the end and through it all, God will win back most of His creation and that those who honor Him to the best of *their* revelation are redeemed.

Knowing the extent of God's goodness will strengthen our faith and cement our conviction that, in the words of the old folks, "God is truly better to us than we are to ourselves." God's goodness further suggests that despite all the fascinating theologies and theories, and not a few ominous and creative conclusions about God, you and I are not in jeopardy of being doomed to hell if we don't "get it" or select the right beliefs.

God is not only good, but He is also a faithful and loving Father. There is more to be known than any religion can tell. After all, the Bible says clearly in John 21:25, "Now, there are many other things that Jesus did. If they were all written down one by one, I suppose that the whole world could not hold the books that would be written" (GNT).

The glory of the book of John is seen not only in his keen conclusion of Jesus' expansive deeds too numerous to mention, but also in his powerful revelation that Jesus is the Lamb of God whose blood sacrifice takes away the sins of the world. That includes you. That includes me. That includes religion. Could God be this good?

So relax. Don't be afraid of knowing how good God is. And don't get mired in what may be a legitimate biblical discussion of His judgment. Don't get it twisted. God is a God of righteousness, holiness, and judgment; however, resist the natural human religious tendency to love judgment more than mercy.

Loving mercy is not the characteristic of a spiritual wimp or religious liberal. Micah 6:8 says, "He has shown you, O man, what is good; and what does the LORD require of you but to do justly, to love mercy, and to walk humbly with your God?" (NKJV). I mean, come on! Really? It's okay to love mercy. God says it is so.

We're talking about the omnipotent God here. I assure you, no one will sneak past the guards at the gate (there are cameras everywhere). I also take modest comfort in His Word that says the way will be made so plain "wayfaring men, though fools, shall not err therein" (Isa. 35:8 KJV), and He is "not willing that *any* should perish" (2 Pet. 3:9 NKJV, emphasis added). Those and countless other scriptures point to a God who may be better than you've been taught.

So given His Word, His wisdom, and His way, I can announce here and now that the preponderance of the evidence shows that in the end God and His kingdom win. It won't even be close. He's that good.

CHAPTER 3

GOD WINS

I looked up and saw a white horse standing there. Its rider carried a bow, and a crown was placed on his head. He rode out to win many battles and gain the victory.
—REVELATION 6:2 (NLT)

Personal Epiphany

An epiphany, according to *Encarta World English Dictionary*, is a "sudden intuitive leap of understanding, especially through an ordinary but striking occurrence." I have had three epiphanies in my encounters with God that have helped form the matrix of my personal growth and understanding and over time profoundly challenged and changed me, ultimately leading to writing this book. I must confess that these experiences were framed by an insatiable curiosity to know how it was possible for God to save the whole world; and if God was who I was taught He was—all-powerful, all-knowing, always present everywhere, eternal, sovereign, holy, just, and good—how could He lose most of His creation to the devil and end up with only a remnant who favor Him?

God Is Fair

My first experience happened at the tender age of fourteen (I refer you to the introduction of this book). My early curiosity about fairness and justice led me to question the implications of my Christian Sunday school training that seemed to imply that because of my good fortune to be born in the right country to the right parents who stumbled upon the right denomination and attended the right congregation, I therefore had the opportunity to learn about Jesus. What about the children and adults who were born in the deep bush lands of my native Africa or the faraway nooks and crannies of China? What would happen to all those people who died never having heard about Jesus?

Mama's answer made me love God long before I officially accepted Him as my personal Lord and Savior. "Don't worry, she said. "I believe God is fair and just and has figured all that out." From that day to this, I have pondered and wondered if God could really be that good. From that day forward, I grew up with the secret belief that we all would be all right because somehow God was going to save us all—even some of the people I thought were bad. Whatever else God was, I believed He was fair. The fix was in; He was the winner. Calm down - everything was going to be okay.

I realize how naïve that sounds, but I grew up with an earthly daddy who could fix anything, so I just believed my heavenly Father—the one who created my daddy, everybody else, and everything else—could and would fix all the stuff Adam had broken.

I Love You

My second experience happened one Monday morning in 1972 in Hanford, California, when I was the guest evangelist for an annual camp meeting. It was hot, over ninety degrees even at 2:00 a.m. I was up late, preparing the message and worrying over one of my least favorite scriptures, Isaiah 64:6: "But we are all as an unclean thing, and all our righteousness are as filthy rags; and we all do fade as a leaf; and our iniquities, like the wind, have taken us away" (KJV).

As I pondered the passage, I heard a gentle voice call my name and ask me a question: "Tyrone, do you know why I love you?" Before I could answer, He spoke again: "Do you think I love you because, in the name of your holiness doctrine, you preach against women wearing pants? Would you give jewelry more power than you give My blood?" It was my Savior speaking, and He was shaming me. The paper I was making notes on became a blur as my eyes began to fill with tears. He spoke again: "I love you for you, not for your standards or for your stands on the doctrine of holiness." (I think He really wanted to say "your extreme stands," but I was already a blubbering mess, so He let it go.)

My tears became a full-blown snotty cry as I realized God wanted my relationship not my righteousness. I tried to speak, but all that would come out was "I'm sorry… I'm so sorry." I have since learned that whenever God shows up like that, He brings clarity with Him. This exchange went on for some time; I was caught up in a new kind of repentance. I felt I had been the spokesman for religious pettiness, and in zealous ignorance, I had minimized the precious blood of Jesus. In the sanctity and silence of that moment, I noted that my repentance was not driven by guilt or fear, but by love for the Savior.

That camp meeting week, I preached from the heart of God about His awesome love and grace. I was born… again. After ten years of being saved and filled with His Holy Spirit, after eight years of preaching and pastoring, I was in love with my Lord for the first time in my life. I loved Him, having discovered His unbridled and unconditional love for me. It was the beginning of a spiritual evolution.

When I returned home to my congregation, before launching into the sermon that first Sunday, I shared my revelation and apologized for presenting a hard, harsh gospel that promoted judgment over mercy. It was as if a chain had been broken. I was beginning to know God by His love, not just by His law. It would take years before I could completely divest myself of the toxic extremes of my upbringing. Even now, I am still an unfinished work, but He who began this good work in me will complete it before the day of Jesus Christ.

I Don't Lose

My third experience took me to yet another level. I was sitting on the front row in Power Center Church International, preparing to bring the Word. The place was packed and "popp'n." I mean, it was on! The people were rejoicing, and the gifts of the Spirit were flowing. In the words of the late Bishop Benjamin F. Reid, "They looked like they were going to go to heaven with their clothes on"—right from where they were. They were dancing, shouting, leaping, weeping, and running. Suddenly, underneath that din of praise, I heard His voice. I heard Him.

Just as He had done the second time, He called me by my middle name: "Tyrone… [a little three-second pause] I don't lose… [another pause]. Do you know who died on the cross? *God died on the cross.*" My mind exploded. As I've said before, when God visits like that He brings with Him clarity. It was instantaneous. I knew exactly what He was saying to me.

"God was reconciling the world to himself in Christ, not counting men's sins against them" (2 Cor. 5:19). God came down from heaven to save the world. God incarnate, God in the flesh,

God Emmanuel ("with us"), who would be called Jesus, came to bail out His creation—all of it.

He said it again: "I don't lose," followed by, "It won't be close. The score will be quintillion to fourteen." You want to know something funny? I didn't even know *quintillion* was a real number. I thought it merely emphasized what God was saying to me. I instinctively assumed it was figurative and simply meant a huge score. I took for granted it was a made-up number, not a real one.

When I typed in what I had heard, however, I noticed the spell-checker didn't highlight it, which meant it was a real word. So I looked it up and found that *quintillion* is ten with eighteen zeros behind it: 10^{18}, or 10,000,000,000,000,000,000. My mouth was open, and tears streamed down my cheeks again. Revelation came so fast I didn't know what to do. In that prophetic moment I was assured that God will win the battle for the souls of humanity.

I absolutely and instantly understood what He meant. It was not really about a score but about a principle. The cross was the fulfillment of the grand strategy designed in eternity before the world began and prophesied in the realm of time in Genesis 3:15. Jesus' death paid the penalty for everybody's sin—past, present, and future. According to Romans 5:8, He paid for our sin while we were still in our sin:

> God commendeth His love toward us, in that, while
> we were yet sinners, Christ died for us. (ASV)

Now here's the mind-blowing glorious truth of Romans 5:8: our sins were paid forward. They were paid before they were ever committed. In the words of the Negro spiritual, "Ain't a-that good news?" God did not die for His creation just to allow the adversary to steal, kill, and destroy it; to divide it into races, religions, and nationalities; to conquer it. Before the foundation of the world,

He prophesied He would save us, and that is exactly what He did. Hallelujah, what a Savior! God won at the cross—not at the altar. Justification was accomplished at the cross not the altar. It was "finished" at the cross, not the altar.

God's Secret Weapon and Winning Strategy

When I remember that God's strategy to save His creation was not done on the fly or created as a counterpunch to a left hook thrown by Satan, I sigh in relief and rejoice that He had me in mind before I had a mind. The battle for the hearts and souls of His creation was programmed and choreographed in eternity. There was a prepared answer to every question, a preconceived solution to every problem, and a perfect accounting for every variable that in the realm of time appeared spontaneous, but in the realm of eternity was expected, planned, and worked according to divine order and purpose.

The question then becomes, how does the omniscient God win against the out-of- control free will of man? I'm glad you asked. I believe that when God made man in His image, that image included characteristics that would always link them. The psalmist describes it as deep calling unto deep (Psalm. 42:7). The most powerful characteristic of God is His love. God *is* love, and that love calls to the deep of man's soul. Like a computer chip embedded in the human psyche, like a homing beacon in the soul, God's love calls out to Himself. This love implant triggers man's "want to" and calls back of its own free will. And at that instant, God wins. God wins at the point of a person's "want to." The body contaminated by every imaginable sin groans for redemption and waits for the pollution of this life to be lifted by the deliverance back to its source.

Consider this powerful thought:

> For we know that the whole creation groans and labors with birth pangs together until now. Not only that, but we also who have the first fruits of the Spirit, even we ourselves groan within ourselves, eagerly waiting for the adoption, the redemption of our body.
>
> —ROMANS 8:22–23 (NKJV)

Now read the same passage from the Amplified Bible:

> We know that the whole creation [of irrational creatures] has been moaning together in the pains of labor until now. And not only the creation, but we ourselves too, who have and enjoy the first fruits of the [Holy] Spirit [a foretaste of the blissful things to come] groan inwardly as we wait for the redemption of our bodies [from sensuality and the grave, which will reveal] our adoption (our manifestation as God's sons).

Something in us makes us groan for God, causes us to long for our eternal home, and triggers us to want God of our own free will. Like a homing pigeon, our hearts head for home even when we have lost our way. We are drawn back to a love that very few can resist. It is the siren call of the soul for a love like no other. As Ecclesiastes 3:10–11 says,

> I have seen the painful labor and exertion and miserable business which God has given to the sons of men with which to exercise and busy themselves. He has made everything beautiful in its time. He also has planted eternity in men's hearts and minds [a divinely implanted sense of a purpose working through the ages which nothing under the sun but God alone can satisfy], yet so that men cannot find out what God has done from the beginning to the end. (AMP)

Love is God's secret weapon and winning strategy. Man's free will responds to love even when that will is twisted and demented, and in spite of cultural circumstances or conditions. Whether a person is drug addicted or suicidal, perpetrator or victim, the desire for God is awakened, and the blood of God is His get-out-of-jail-free card. Satan, competing for the will of man, loses to the love of God, for there is no greater love than God's love. God wins.

I am reminded of one of my favorite hymns, "Love Lifted Me" written by James Rowe in 1912,

> I was sinking deep in sin far, from the peaceful shore;
> Very deeply stained within, I was sinking to rise no more.
> But the Master of the sea heard my despairing cry [Jesus!]
> And from the waters lifted me, now safe am I.
>
> Chorus:
> Love lifted me!
> Love lifted me!
> When nothing else could help,
> Love lifted me!
> Love lifted me!
> Love lifted me!
> When nothing else could help,
> Love lifted me.

Satan, the devil, the enemy of the soul of man—or whatever else you want to call him—has no defense against the love of God. His only weapon is fear—fear that God is out to get us; fear that humankind's sins are greater than God's grace; fear that only some, not all, will be saved; fear of the unknown; fear of the unknowable; fear of being wrong.

I am also made confident in the knowledge that God's first idea is His final decision. He's that good. To use a basketball analogy, He always shoots His best shot first. He shoots three-pointers from the corner or center court, and He beats the buzzer every time. He's good! He is spectacular in form and function. He steals victory out of the jaws of certain defeat. Dang, He's good!

He is unrehearsed and unscripted. He has only a plan A. There is no plan B because He's that good. True to form, He didn't send to the earth Gabriel or Michael, the mighty archangels who stand day and night in the presence of El Shaddai, God Almighty. He came down Himself. God incarnate—Emmanuel, "God with Us"—came in the form of Jesus.

> And the Word was made flesh, and dwelt among us, (and we beheld his glory, the glory as of the only begotten of the Father,) full of grace and truth.
> —JOHN 1:14 (KJV)

He went to the cross, having overcome every temptation and every power on earth. Qualifying as the perfect sacrifice, God the Son shouted with a voice of triumph heard in heaven and hell—"It is finished" (John 19:30). And in an instant, He became the perfect Savior and greatest champion.

"It is finished" is the translation of the Greek term *tetelestai*. This is the perfect indicative mood of the Greek verb *teleō*, which means "to bring to an end" or "to complete." The mood and tense of a verb indicate the attitude of the speaker, and Jesus' grammar reveals the following: (1) the perfect tense means the action was completed in the past with results continuing into the present. Translation: It *was* finished then, and it *is* finished now. (2) The indicative mood shows that the act that took place or the condition is an objective fact. Translation: The work that Jesus finished was definite and real. Furthermore, Jesus spoke in the (3) passive voice, which indicates He was receiving or was being subjected to an action without responding or initiating a response.

Translation: The work that Jesus did was passive in the sense that His dying love was unconditional! ("A Word Study of John 19:30"; Helpmewithbiblestudy.org., 2009)

Bam—that's the one! The passive voice suggests no action is required. To the devil, that's a humiliating in-your-face, ain't-nothin'-you-can-do-about-it slam dunk! To the sinner, the passive voice of "It is finished" proclaims, "Now get up and put your clothes on. Daddy says, 'Come on home.' He's not holding this mess against you" (see 2 Corinthians 5:19). How awesome is it to have your daddy as your judge?

"It is finished" was not said in a weak last breath. Jesus saved His best for last. *"Tetelestai!"* It was the shout of the winner. It was a vicious slam-dunk buzzer beater that won the game. It was the shout of one thrusting a sword into the heart of an enemy. *"Tetelestai!* Mission accomplished! Debt paid in full!" It was God settling the score and forever satisfying the claim of justice.

God the Son committed His spirit to God the Father, who found no fault in Him. He was thus legally free to reverse the curse of humankind on whose behalf He died. Get this—God died! The eternal Father came from eternity to pay a debt that had stalked humanity since Adam's fall. This victory was prophesied in Genesis 3:15. As promised, it was paid forward. The debt is now paid, and nothing is owed. What is left is quality of life; an invading kingdom of righteousness, peace, and joy; a Believer's lifestyle of unconditional love that, I believe, is the best way to get you home with the fewest number of bruises and scars.

On the Winning Side

It took some changing on my part in order for me to join the winning team. In the beginning, I was more church oriented than kingdom oriented. I represented my denomination in theological debates about the doctrine of eternal security versus the Holiness doctrine of sinless perfection. It took a while, but over time I evolved from a narrow parochial mind-set that worried only about the advancement of my Christian denomination to a kingdom worldview that included far more than my small Christian denomination. I no longer concern myself about non-Christian believers being accepted by God; after all, it's His heaven. While I remain committed to sharing my Christocentric perspective, I am not committed to arguing to the death the perspective of others. I fully embrace the ancient proverb attributed to the German theologian Rupertus Meldenius: "In essentials, unity; in nonessentials, liberty; and in all things, charity." I am committed to loving like Jesus. I have found it to be the best strategy for winning others to a Godly lifestyle.

I began to change perspectives from religion to relationship after I was drafted into the U. S. Army. In the army, I met men who loved God like I did (and a few who seemed to love Him more—that was really unnerving), but whose theology and doctrine were very different from mine. It soon became apparent to me that either I had to adjust some of my beliefs, or everybody except me was going to hell. That realization led to the frightening conclusion that maybe some of the stuff I believed in and argued about was not all that important or true… or, in some cases, neither important nor true.

I soon discovered that the winning strategy was not the finger-pointing "you're going to hell if you don't believe what I believe" strategy, but rather, the demonstration of God's Spirit and the power of His love. It was God's love and compassion that won me to Him and made me a citizen of His kingdom, and it would be God's love and compassion through me that would best influence others, not necessarily to a specific religion, but to a relationship with God.

God Wins

For me, the greatest mystery is not how most people will be saved, but rather how anyone could end up lost and in hell, given that their rescuer and savior is the sovereign God whose power is absolute and arbitrary. He is Jehovah—"I am that I am"—and He is called Jehovah YHWH, which means, "The I Am Who Is the Almighty." Tell me, please, how do you escape Jehovah's love if He wants to love you? How does the Creator God, Elohim, not win the battle of wills if He can change the heart of the king (Proverbs 21:1), if He can flip the will of a dying thief (Luke 23:42), if He has willed that no man should perish but that all should come to repentance (2 Peter 3:9)? Tell me again, how does one escape such a God? I tell you again, the score will be quintillion to… maybe… one hundred or so. In other words, it won't even be close. The Almighty One will have the last word, and Jehovah, the King of Kings, has already made the last move. On the third day, Jesus got up—checkmate, game, set, match. God wins!

According to Romans 14:17, the kingdom of God is not physical—it is spiritual. It is righteousness, peace, and joy, and the Bible is clear that I am included: "Not by works of righteousness which we have done, but according to his mercy he saved us" (Titus 3:5 KJV). And it is crystal clear that Jesus (God in the flesh) is my righteousness, for the Word says, "This is his name whereby he shall be called, THE LORD OUR RIGHTEOUSNESS" (Jeremiah. 23:6 KJV). John 14:27 says He is my peace, John 15:11 says He is my joy, and 1 John 4:16 says He is love. He wins His creation back with a strategy of unrelenting, unsurpassing, undeniable, unfathomable, and unconditional love. Could God be this good?

CHAPTER 4

THE STRUGGLE FOR SIMPLICITY

*And a highway shall be there, and it shall be called the
Way of Holiness; the unclean shall not pass over it. It
shall belong to those who walk on the way; even if they
are fools, they shall not go astray.*

—ISAIAH 35:8 (ESV)

Theologies and Theories

A general rule I follow regarding philosophies, perspectives,
theories, and theologies is this: if it comes from man, whether
inspired or not, it is open for discussion. All the theologies and
theories notwithstanding, the Bible's teachings about the character
and nature of God belie many of the traditional and emerging
theologies and theories of well-intentioned scholars.

It is helpful but not necessary for good Christians to accept
the Bible as the infallible Word of God in order to understand and
believe in Jesus' teachings of universal compassion. After all, the
early Christians did not possess a Bible, either infallible or faulty,
to carry around with them. It wasn't even compiled until centuries

later. Just as we gain insights and understanding from modern writers and commentators without claiming that they are divine or infallible, we can also gain insight and understanding from ancient writers, as long as we consider their works for what they are, inspired but human, and allow critical thinking and common sense to prevail over theological and denominational prejudice, predisposition, and blind faith in fallible human conviction.

It is my faith in God, Jehovah, El Shaddai—not in what man thinks, theologizes, theorizes, philosophizes, or preaches—that gives me hope, moral and spiritual purpose, meaning, and strength. My relationship with God is more important than my understanding of the rules. Yes, the letter indeed kills, but the Spirit gives life. Ultimately, "God is" is enough for me, thank you very much—I'll take it from there. The parallel and the paradoxical truths; the brilliant intellectual contrasts and comparisons; the gaps and absence of historical fact, information, and understanding; the parochial time-based logic, presumptions, assumptions, surmisings, and private interpretations; and the debate of whether there be other earths, universes, and galaxies with human-type life forms, theologies, and so on - make it relatively easy for me to believe and rest in two things: (1) in the beginning, God; and (2) it is finished.

God fixed it and finished it: the salvation of man—*done*. That pretty much summarizes my personal theology, religious theory, and religious philosophy. Said another way: God said it, I believe it, and that settles it! Keep in mind, though, I believe my *believing it* is not required for *it* to be settled.

Consequently, though at times my observations may appear to favor one side or another, or sometimes a little of both, I refuse to take a fixed position in complicated theological discourse and debate or to allow any argument to close my mind to any other argument. I have come to a rather broad understanding—and I would dare say *revelation*—that is the foundational premise of this book. And that is that Jehovah God, Yahweh, Yeshua, is far bigger and greater than the millennia and countless volumes of human speculation about Him.

The Legacy of Adam's Fall

Adam left a legacy of pathological self-centered human predisposition. As the human race, we were left too damaged to be trusted, in an absolute sense, for spiritual and eternal answers. Consequently, the plan of salvation does not depend on human participation to be successful.

The Bible teaches that Adam's sin of disobedience contaminated the entire human race. I would suggest that Adam and the whole of humanity not only inherited the DNA of sin and its curse of death as a consequence, but even more importantly inherited a narcissistic spirit as a direct spin-off of Adam's fall.

By *narcissistic spirit*, I am suggesting that the fall of Adam and Eve launched the "me" era that has corrupted all humanity, especially leaders in all categories both secular and religious. Key to the satanic temptation of Adam and Eve was the suggestion that they would become as God (see Genesis 3). The implication was simple but deadly: if you are equal to God, you don't need God, and "I" takes center stage.

Adam and Eve traded their connection with God and the endless power and privilege it represented for the possibility of equality and independence they hoped would come with disconnection. They wanted life to be about them. They wanted center stage. They wanted control of their destinies.

Instead, they immediately discovered that disconnection from their life source brought the promised death; and with disconnection and death, limitation, a ticking clock, a learning curve, and ever-present lust rose to the center. Without the advantage of unlimited partnership with Jehovah Elohim, the God of creation, they were forced to evolve, or grow over time. Now they had to learn by trial and error what they would have known by connection. Because of the disconnection, they now had to compete with a natural environment that was no longer automatically submitted to them because of divine connection and delegated dominion.

Adam and Eve's decision to disobey was fueled by their desire to be independent, to be self-controlled, to make self the center. And that, my friends, is the nasty subtle legacy of Adam's sin: humankind replaced God as the center of all things. From the moment of Adam's disobedience to this very day, the lasting legacy of sin in the flesh is the new instinct to be the center.

Someone has said, "The trouble with sin is its middle letter." The *I* in sin represents independence. It contaminates everything man touches, speaks or does. In almost every attempt at organizing for the common good, some narcissistic, egotistical individual seeks to exploit the common good for his own self-aggrandizing purpose. He anoints himself king, emperor, pope, or whatever and makes himself the center. It is the legacy of Adam's fall.

Why is this important? It helps to explain why God's strategy for the world could never depend on anyone but God Himself. Governments, kingdoms, nations, and religions are all affected and infected spin-offs of this legacy. All disunity is a spin-off of original sin, and we all struggle to understand God through minds that have evolved from this ancient and deadly disconnection.

Most of our greatest Judeo-Christian heroes and leaders, from Abraham, the father of faith; to Moses, the law giver and deliverer; to King David, the greatest king of the Jews and the man after God's own heart; to theologians, scholars, popes, television evangelists, powerful preachers, and pastors of mega-churches, have all been scarred by personal and public failure whose cause leads back to selfish ambition, self-preservation, and the narcissistic lust for the center.

Our best efforts to reconnect to the God whose image imprints us is contaminated by the side effects of this original sin, which presents the classic battle between spirit and flesh described by the apostle Paul in Romans 7:14–25 (NIV):

> We know that the law is spiritual; but I am unspiritual, sold as a slave to sin. I do not understand what I do. For what I want to do I do not do, but what I hate I do. And if I do what I do not want to do, I agree that the law is good. As it is, it is no longer I myself who do it, but it is sin living in me. For I know that good itself does not dwell in me, that is, in my sinful nature. For I have the desire to do what is good, but I cannot carry it out. For I do not do the good I want to do, but the evil I do not want to do—this I keep on doing. Now if I do what I do not want to do, it is no longer I who do it, but it is sin living in me that does it.
>
> So I find this law at work: Although I want to do good, evil is right there with me. For in my inner being I delight in God's law; but I see another law at work in me, waging war against the law of my mind and making me a prisoner of the law of sin at work within me. What a wretched man I am! Who will rescue me from this body that is subject to death? Thanks be to God, who delivers me through Jesus Christ our Lord! So then, I myself in my mind am a slave to God's law, but in my sinful nature a slave to the law of sin.

Given man's post-Eden instinct to put himself in the center, is it any wonder God's strategy for saving humankind was exclusively

His act? Thus it gives me great pleasure to proclaim that no single religion, no denomination, no preacher, no theology, no tradition, no ceremony, no ritual, no rite, and no interpretation will determine who is saved and who is not. Our arrogant, self-righteous arguments about which religious system or doctrine is right or wrong serves no redeeming purpose in God's grand strategy of love. Such judgments are a waste of time and credibility and, again, places man in the center. Salvation is of the Lord. We are called to be ambassadors of the message of reconciliation – only.

Forest and Trees Revisited

Understanding God is an oxymoron. The creature can never fully understand the creator, nor can he hope to fully explain what he cannot fully understand. Though time cannot comprehend eternity, we humans possess an insatiable curiosity about our origin and our end, the meaning and purpose of our lives, and where we go from here.

In our attempt to understand human existence, we research and analyze our own findings in microscopic detail. After our best scholarship and the parsing and reparsing of words, concepts, and conclusions, we are left with one of two things: belief or unbelief. Either we believe our own time-based finite findings or we believe God's revelation of Himself. There are times we can't see the forest for looking at the trees. Chasing the proverbial "truth rabbits" takes us in ever-widening circles that always lead us back to where we started and, more often than not, with more questions than when we began.

For example, while researching the commentary on Genesis 3:15, a passage I know from memory and one I have preached from many times, I learned a new term: *protoevangelium*, or "first gospel." Up until then, I had always taught that this verse was simply the first messianic prophecy, but *protoevangelium* suggests an even wider understanding. As one source says, "Not only was this the first messianic prophecy, but this passage coming on the heels of man's greatest sin (his first sin) suggests 'good news' was coming with the Savior" (Biblescripture.net/First.html). Since the whole universe had just been cast into chaos, the only news that would be good news would be the coming of a Savior who would bring with Him order.

Okay, I can handle *protoevangelium*, but the author is not finished. He goes on to suggest a relationship between Genesis and the Torah and that the presence of the epicene personal pronoun as being significant in the dating of the Pentateuch:

> This use of an epicene personal pronoun—one pronoun for both "he" and "she"—signifies ancient Hebrew and was also seen in original Phoenician and Moabite manuscripts as well. (Biblescripture.net)

Now I'm irritated. Genesis 3 in general, and verse 15 in particular, will never be the same. In an instant, the commentator goes from simple to complex. I see no reason for this involved explanation, except perhaps to teach seminary students how to research and do higher critical religious philosophy... maybe. But I declare to you, Joe Blow who works on the assembly line at Ford Motor Company in Livonia, Michigan, could not care less. Perhaps I have fallen victim to intellectual "ghetto creep" - that knee-jerk reaction to red tape, big words and intellectual concepts.

My point, albeit tortured, is that scholars have had millenniums to complicate simple things, which in turn become self-aggrandizing, self-perpetuating, self-consuming, and self-serving. In the meantime, they could make life simple, as does this unknown author who closes a brilliant lesson on Genesis 3:15 with the following summary:

Genesis 3:15 is a promise, a message of hope for mankind. God created this world and retains dominion over the world. God will not let the force of evil prevail, but will deliver mankind from its grip... The expulsion of Adam and Eve from the Garden of Eden is mitigated by hope of an offspring of the woman. (Biblescripture.net;Cardinal Joseph Ratzinger et al;Proto-Evangelium;Theological Summary)

Yes! Now we're talkin'! I must be careful, however, not to cast disparaging shadows over the hard work of scholars who have spent their lifetimes digging for information that verifies the human theories about God, casts more doubt and confusion or raises new questions. But sometimes I just want to scream, "Keep it simple!"

So, no matter who you are and what religion you are—serious, weird, or otherwise— you have a fighting chance because of the death and resurrection of God through His Son Jesus. There is no other name under heaven by which man can be saved. However, that singular act of God, His sacrificial death on the cross, impacts more than Christianity. It impacts the world. It is not being a Christian that saves—it is being reconciled to God that saves, and that reconciliation was accomplished on the cross when He proclaimed, "It is finished!" It is as simple as that. Those words came from God, our Savior, our Yeshua. We who believe those words could be more correctly called Yeshuaites, or Yeshuaians, or some other derivative of God's name – point being, it doesn't matter what the believer is called.

Ultimately, God's act to save humankind must be accepted as a sovereign and supreme act that exceeds our ability to interpret or understand completely. We bring God down to our level when we limit the work of salvation to human participation, interpretation, and understanding.

Romans 5:18 describes what God has done for the world in spite of itself:

> Therefore as by the offence of one judgment came upon all men to condemnation; even so by the righteousness of one the free gift came upon all men unto justification of life. (KJV)

The Message Bible says it this way:

> Here it is in a nutshell: Just as one person did it wrong and got us in all this trouble with sin and death, another person did it right and got us out of it. But more than just getting us out of trouble, he got us into life! One man said no to God and put many people in the wrong; one man said yes to God and put many in the right.

Romans 5:18 is one of the most wonderful passages known or unknown to man. The law of gravity exists whether you believe it or know about it. And the saving act of God on the cross that "came upon all men unto justification of life" is true whether you know it or believe it. *Tetelestai*, "it is finished," "debt paid in full" was not conditioned on man's knowledge or belief. It was prophesied from the beginning in Genesis 3:15. It was fulfilled on the cross of Calvary on approximately April 11, AD 32, according to the Elephantine Papyri.

When God said, "It is finished," it was finished for everybody, including those of us who were yet unborn and who had not yet sinned. Now if that is considered inclusiveness, then so be it. The act of God precedes and supersedes the human error of interpretation. If John 3:16 is considered universalism, then so be it. The act of God precedes, supersedes, and withstands the error and the terror of human interpretation, religious labeling, and all theological parsing. God is that good! He will not squeak out a victory. He's God! He wins in a landslide.

The song "More Than Wonderful" by Lanny Wolfe (1984) and made famous by the awesome duo of Sandi Patty and Larnelle Harris says it like this:

> I stand amazed when I think that the King of glory
> Should come to dwell within the heart of man
> I marvel just to know He really loves me
> When I think of who He is, and who I am.

Sadly, though God is more than wonderful, we humans must deal with the less than wonderful assessments of Him and each other. Until He returns to claim us in spite of our ignorance concerning Him, we will be fighting about Him like fussing siblings each declaring the other is adopted.

Competing Heresies

I have read many theology books and studied many theological perspectives, and I have also taught Bible doctrine and theology. In all these arenas, I have yet to find one subject on which everybody agrees. Moreover, I have found there is usually someone somewhere who thinks that someone else's perspective is heresy. In fact, I have observed that the strength of theological disagreement generally stems from the gaps and voids that leave a subject open to speculation. Since no one has seen God at any time (1 John 4:12), furious and fictional arguments arise from biblical silence, giving every wannabe scholar or preacher the opportunity to weigh in with both public and private interpretations creating a crossfire of competing heresy charges.

One scholar, Gary A. Hand, suggests the ancient Arminian-Calvinist debate is an example of competing heresies and is found in the battle between Arminian and Calvinist theologies. The teaching of Jacobus Arminius came about as a result of his belief that the teachings of John Calvin, with respect to the role of God in salvation, were not correct. Although he had previously been a supporter of Calvin and had accepted the Dutch Reformed doctrines of the absolute sovereignty of God in salvation, predestination and foreordination, he changed his mind and taught against those beliefs. Chief among his beliefs was the idea that man chooses God of his own free will. He believed that man was affected by original sin and could not choose God in that condition, but that God grants to the individual a special grace that removes the effect of the fall and allows the person to make a choice of their own free will.

Arminian theology is a continuation or refinement of Pelagianism, the doctrine of the 5th century English Catholic monk. Jacobus Arminius would deny that he was a proponent of Pelagian heresy, because he did not teach against the concept of original sin, as did Pelagius, but the fact remains that the two schools of belief are very similar and ultimately lead to the same actions by believers. The doctrinal error in Arminianism is that it substitutes an act of man that is of greater authority than the sovereignty of God and makes God subservient to the actions of man rather than man subservient to the actions of God.

Many denominations and sects have adopted the Arminian position, including John and Charles Wesley who founded the Methodist church, most Pentecostal and charismatic churches, Assembly of God, Nazarene, Mennonite, Christian and Missionary Alliance and many Baptist groups. Gary Hand says, "There is a battle going on within the church over the issue that has intensified recently, as the emphasis and belief in the centrality of man over the absolute sovereignty of God has become more prevalent in the theology of the church." (Gary A. Hand; On Doctrine.com; 2001)

I was shocked to discover that Arminianism, whose side I thought I was on theologically, was considered heresy by the Calvinists, whom I considered the well - represented competition. Until recently I didn't know that these two large divisions of Christian believers, each sincere about their beliefs, considered the other a heretic. I thought we were each other's loyal opposition, both Christian, but from different perspectives—but heretic? At first, that seemed to me a serious charge. I was a sinless-perfection, holiness-believing Christian. I thought my belief came from the Bible. In my experience, no one in Sunday school or from the pulpit had ever mentioned the name Jacobus Arminius or John Calvin as founders of the doctrines we believed or disbelieved. In fact, some of the men of God I came up under never formally studied theology or even knew of these theologians, not to mention the historical battle between the two schools of thought.

While in Bible college, I engaged in many debates with my fundamentalist Baptist brothers, whom I loved and respected greatly. We broke bread together before, during, and after intense debates over the doctrines of sinless perfection versus eternal security. However, I never thought them to be heretics— misinformed maybe, but never with the dreaded label of heretic.

The point is, I believe that God is bigger than our zealous misunderstandings and our self-righteous charges of heresy. I'm just saying, these human judgments are not final, thank God!

Heresy Defined

According to *The American Heritage Dictionary*, second college edition, *heresy* is defined as "an opinion or doctrine at variance with established religious beliefs, especially dissension from or denial of Roman Catholic dogma by a professed believer or baptized church member." By this definition, one can immediately see the problem: most of the world is heretic. And therein lies the greater problem: while heresy is clearly warned against in Scripture, declarations of heresy come back to the initial definition of "an opinion."

The biblical term for *heresy* comes from the Greek word *hairesis*, which literally translates "act of choosing" (Dictionary. com). *Strong's* defines heresy from the Greek *hairetikos*, which means "disposed to form sects; to choose; have a distinctive opinion" (*Strong's* 141). In his letter to Titus, the apostle Paul wrote, "A man that is an heretick after the first and second admonition reject" (Titus 3:10 KJV). To paraphrase, this verse literally means "a man who has chosen a distinct opinion that is factious and divisive, after two warnings leave him alone."

Interestingly, the apostle does not suggest a punishment or a judgment for the heretic, nor is it suggested in other passages in the New Testament as it relates to a heretic's ultimate end. Paul does suggest in 1 Corinthians 11:19, however, that heresies are inevitable: "For there must be also heresies among you, that they which are approved may be made manifest among you" (KJV). The tone and tenor of most translations clearly reflect the inevitability of divisive opinions, but also reflect that the truth and the leaders who represent that truth, with God's favor, will rise to the top.

Note the phrasing of 1 Corinthians 11:19 in the following translations:

The Message Bible:
"The best that can be said for it is that the testing process will bring truth into the open and confirm it."

Good News Bible:

"(No doubt there must be divisions among you so that the ones who are in the right may be clearly seen.)"

Young's Literal Translation:

"For it behoveth sects also to be among you, that those approved may become manifest among you."

ISV

"Of course, there must be factions among you to show which of you are genuine!"

NIV

"No doubt there have to be differences among you to show which of you have God's approval."

Once again the horror of heresy seems somewhat diminished in these passages. Perhaps this is because God, in His eternal wisdom, foresaw the many twists and turns that human wisdom would take as it sought to know Him and represent Him on the earth and therefore foreordained the periodic raising up of reformers who would act as course correctors.

From Heretic to Hero

Throughout church history, most reformers have been considered heretics by those they sought to reform. Martin Luther is perhaps the most famous example. Martin Luther's opinions—at least according to the scandalous Roman Catholic Church he sought to reform and which at the time had three popes claiming the papacy at the same time—were considered heresy. John Huss was burned at the stake, and the body of his mentor, John Wycliffe, was dug up and burned and the ashes scattered on the

Rhine River. Today, in the Christian church, John Wycliffe and John Huss are universally celebrated as heroic martyrs (Foxe's *Book of Martyrs*) in the Christian church though Wycliffe died a natural death. I can't let this go until I tell you why.

According to Greatsite.com; "English Bible History" the first handwritten English Bible manuscripts were produced in the 1380s by John Wycliffe, an Oxford professor, scholar, and theologian. Wycliffe was well known throughout Europe for his opposition to the teachings of the organized Roman Catholic Church, which he believed to be contrary to the Bible. With the help of his followers, called the Lollards, his assistant Purvey, and many other faithful scribes, Wycliffe produced dozens of English-language manuscript copies of the Scriptures. They were translated from the Latin Vulgate, which was the only source text available to Wycliffe.

The pope was so infuriated by his teachings and his translation of the Bible into English that forty-four years after Wycliffe's death, Pope Martin V ordered the bones to be dug up and burned and scattered in the river!

One of Wycliffe's followers, John Huss, actively promoted Wycliffe's belief that people should be permitted to read the Bible in their own language and should oppose the tyranny of the Roman Church that threatened execution—not expulsion, but execution—to anyone possessing a non-Latin Bible. Huss was burned at the stake in 1415, with Wycliffe's manuscript Bibles used as kindling for the fire. The last words of John Huss were, "In one hundred years, God will raise up a man whose calls for reform cannot be suppressed." Almost exactly a hundred years later in 1517, Martin Luther nailed his famous Ninety-five Theses of heretical theology and crimes of the Roman Catholic Church onto the church door at Wittenberg. The prophecy of Huss had come true.

The Protestant movement ignited by Martin Luther is alive today. John Wycliffe and John Huss are honored with institutions named after them. Wycliffe Bible Translators is a thriving organization that has tasked itself with translating the Bible into every language in the world. After almost seven hundred years, Wycliffe and Huss have gone from being heretics to heroes, proving that one man's reformer is another man's heretic. Reformers once considered heretics and killed because of their stands are today the heroes of our Christian heritage because God is bigger than the religious systems that killed them. Could God be *that* good?

CHAPTER 5

THE GOD OF OUTCASTS
AND FOREIGNERS

*I have other sheep, too, that are not in this sheepfold. I
must bring them also. They will listen to my voice, and
there will be one flock with one shepherd.*
—JOHN 10:16 (NLT)

Sheep from Other Folds

In the interest of full disclosure, permit me to confess that I am
an unapologetic born-again, saved and sanctified, *Christian*
believer. I am hard pressed to say, as do some of my dear friends,
that the Holy Bible contains all the truth, but I do believe all that
is in the Holy Bible is true. By the time you finish reading this
book, I hope you will share my faith and confidence in the truth
of God's Word, particularly as it relates to His commitment to
save the whole world.

I was triumphantly "justified" at the cross of Calvary some
time in April of AD33. I confessed Jesus as Lord and Savior and
became a Christian convert at the altar of the Wisconsin Avenue

Church of God September 1, 1963. Since the initial confession of my sins and the ensuing baptism with the Holy Spirit, I have experienced and am yet experiencing a wonderful transformation and maturation as a human being and as a Christian believer. My transformation has been slow and steady. Doctrinally, I have moved from an extremely conservative view (my way or the highway) to a more moderate one that is willing to listen and tolerate other points of view. My journey has not been without adventure and adversity, but the lessons learned have been invaluable.

In 1969, I was the evangelist for a good old-fashioned revival at the great Liberty Road Church of God in Houston, Texas. After a week of hard preaching, I experienced a visitation of God's presence that changed me forever. On that last Sunday, drunk with the wine of God's anointing, I said, "When we get to heaven, we are going to be shocked to find all denominations represented, even those on the far end of the Christian spectrum. I believe there are going to be Catholics, Jehovah's Witnesses, Lutherans, Episcopalians, Presbyterians, and maybe even some Church of God folks [my own denomination] in heaven." The crowd responded in total agreement, even though this was not a traditional belief of our denomination. But that's what happens when you get caught up in the Spirit: you say things you had not planned to say, and you believe things you did not believe before.

After the preaching had ended and a tremendous altar response was concluded, just before the benediction an elderly man who had pastored about fifteen people for the past forty years stood to his feet, pointed his "sanctified" finger toward the pulpit, and began to rail against my statement about the unity of the body of Christ. He finished his harsh rebuke and sat down.

I didn't know what to say or do. He was my elder, but the Detroit Eastside ghetto in me wanted to respond. I felt a hand on my knee. It was the big strong hand of a widely respected pastor in the state of Texas, Isaac W. Mitchell. His hand stayed me while he rose to his feet.

A tall, gravel-voiced ex-Marine, Pastor Mitchell served in San Antonio, Texas, and he reminded the people that we had just experienced an awesome outpouring of God's Spirit, with signs following. The altar response and the testimonies shared were proof positive, he said, that God had "spoken through this young man." Furthermore, he added, "I absolutely agree with his statement and will not allow anyone to discredit what God has said to us." It was apostolic authority in action.

My eyes were as big as saucers. I sensed this was a watershed moment. A generational shift and a theological reset occurred that allowed the church to broaden its perspective without the guilt that normally follows when tradition is challenged or broken. His words were received with a joyous *amen*. Somehow I sensed this was just one battle, for change must wage many battles before the war is won.

In the euphoria of the moment, I was immediatcly asked to return as guest evangelist for a future special occasion. I accepted the invitation but sometime later received a call from the chairman of the committee. Apologizing, he said, "I was premature with my invitation. I must withdraw it in deference to a few of our older ministers."

I was twenty-four years old and just getting started. I learned quickly the depth and danger of orthodoxy and amazed myself at my own unwillingness to change. However, as time passed, I also learned lessons taught only in the crucible of life itself. Life's experiences will either validate or invalidate one's beliefs. I have since learned that what one believes must be livable in the real world. Time has taught me that good theology is relevant theology. I have learned that we must adjust to both revelation and reality and that we are often faced with the dubious choice to either change or become irrelevant.

Perhaps my greatest challenge has been to reconcile my Christian faith with what I call "non-Christian believers." By *non-Christian believers*, I refer to those who believe and practice precepts and principles about God that closely match those in Christianity. The question then becomes, do the other sheepfolds that Jesus speaks of in John 10:16 include non-Christians? And does "lowering" my standard as it relates to accepting other non-Christian believers make me a compromising Christian in danger of losing my soul? What, exactly, are the other sheepfolds referred to in John 10:16? Who are the sheep in them, where did they come from, and to which one of the more than thirty-three thousand Christian denominations should they convert?

Competing Covenants

A cursory examination of the competing covenants as they relate to Ishmael and Isaac may help us to understand, at least in principle, today's religious divisions and that God's plan of redemption is also their plan; and that they are the other sheep from other sheepfolds that Jesus referenced. First was the covenant between God, Abraham, and Ishmael:

> And as for Ishmael, I have heard thee: Behold, I have blessed him, and will make him fruitful and will multiply him exceedingly; twelve princes shall he beget, and I will make him a great nation.
> —GENESIS 17:20 (KJV)

Second, a similar covenant was established between God, Abraham, and Isaac, who was not the first child, but was the child of promise:

> But my covenant will I establish with Isaac, which
> Sarah shall bear unto thee at this set time in the next
> year.
>
> —Genesis 17:21 (KJV)

Not only was Ishmael the first child of the covenant, but he was also given a divine and prophetic inheritance:

> And the angel of the Lord said unto her, I will multiply
> thy seed exceedingly, that it shall not be numbered for
> multitude… And he will be a wild man; and his hand
> shall be against every man, and every man's hand
> against him; and he shall dwell in the presence of
> all his brethren… And as for Ishmael, I have heard
> thee [Abraham]: Behold, I have blessed him, and will
> make him fruitful, and will multiply him exceedingly;
> twelve princes shall he beget, and I will make him a
> great nation."
>
> —Genesis 16:10, 12; 17:20 (KJV)

Now let's link these scriptures with an even more dramatic declaration to this pre-Islamic son of Abraham and covenant partner with Isaac. Hagar had been banished, sent packing, cast out by her mistress, Sarah. Alone and destitute, as she was preparing to die, God spoke to her:

> And she sat over against him, and lift up her voice, and
> wept. And God heard the voice of the lad [Ishmael]
> and the angel of God called to Hagar out of heaven…
> Hagar fear not; for God has heard the voice of the lad
> where he is… Arise, lift up the lad, and hold him in
> thine hand; for I will make him a great nation… And
> God was with the lad.
>
> —Genesis 21:16–20 (KJV)

It is clear that Ishmael, a covenant child and the progenitor of Islam, and Isaac, the covenant child of promise and the progenitor of Judaism, were both the offspring of Abraham, the father of faith, and were both blessed to be great nations. Some would argue the difference in their greatness, but I would argue the principle of their greatness. I would argue that unlike their purpose and destiny, their difference is irrelevant. The omniscient Jehovah activated these great nations, knowing that He, Jehovah/Allah, would come to the earth in person and die to save them both.

I have concluded that I will be satisfied with whatever satisfies the Creator, not the creatures. I believe that every man, woman, boy, and girl will see and celebrate the revelation of God, some according to the letter and some according to the spirit of the letter because Jesus—without their permission, knowledge, or understanding—has revealed Him (God) in the earth, and that revelation is manifested to all, even overcoming their religious filters.

Romans 1:16–23 in the Message Bible says it this way:

> It's news I'm most proud to proclaim, this extraordinary Message of God's powerful plan to rescue everyone who trusts him, starting with Jews and then right on to everyone else! God's way of putting people right shows up in the acts of faith, confirming what Scripture has said all along: The person in right standing before God by trusting him really lives.

> But God's angry displeasure erupts as acts of human mistrust and wrongdoing and lying accumulate, as people try to put a shroud over truth. But the basic reality of God is plain enough. Open your eyes and there it is! By taking a long and thoughtful look at what God has created, people have always been able to see what their eyes as such can't see: eternal power,

for instance, and the mystery of his divine being. So nobody has a good excuse. What happened was this: People knew God perfectly well, but when they didn't treat him like God, refusing to worship him, they trivialized themselves into silliness and confusion so that there was neither sense nor direction left in their lives.

These are words that assure us of the faithfulness of God to reveal Himself. I believe that all humankind will see Him one way or another, and all will be held accountable for what they believe about Him. Accountability is reflected in the quality of their lives, which will be in direct proportion to their pursuit of Him and obedience to their revelation of Him and the destiny of their souls will be assured by the same finished work of Jesus.

God Is a Spirit

All over the world, men and women are awakened to a consciousness of God. Where they are in the world determines how they define their consciousness of God. They instinctively try to worship whatever it is that has awakened them. They name Him according to their language and interpretation of their revelation in the context of their experience and environment. They honor and fear and devise ways and rituals to win favor from what or whom they honor and fear. Perhaps He is God Jehovah if they are in Africa, Asia, or Europe; or Allah if they are in Africa or the Middle East; or maybe Chac, the Mayan name for Him; or Viracocha, the name given to Him by the Inca Indians, which means "The Lord—the Omnipotent Creator of All Things" (Don Richardson, *Eternity in Their Hearts,* Regal Books, revised 1984, p. 39). But whatever He is called in whatever language He is named, He is above them, mightier than they and worthy of worship. Again, this is the simple understanding of Romans 1:19–20:

> Since what may be known about God is plain to them, because God has made it plain to them. For since the creation of the world God's invisible qualities—his eternal power and divine nature—have been clearly seen, being understood from what has been made, so that people are without excuse.

Could this explain how the one act of God, Jesus' death on the cross, covers every man, woman, boy, and girl in the world? After all, the Word says, "God is a Spirit: and they that worship him must worship him in spirit and in truth" (John 4:24 KJV). When the Native American Indians prayed to the Great Spirit, were they closer to getting it right than some of us? Were they at least as right as those with biblical revelation? Without the benefit of the Word that helps explain to whom they were praying, were they already in contact and serving the God who is the *Holy Spirit*?

Clearly, if God gave competing covenants between relatives, I can accept the ecumenical mystery of competing religions and their inevitable reconciliation. In the meantime, we struggle to understand how these religions will ever be compatible—or need they be? A cursory summary of some of the leading religions suggests only that God knows how He will bring them into one fold. What I am sure about is that Jesus' death and resurrection has paved the way for the salvation of the whole world. *How* God brings them to a saving faith is known only to their Righteous Judge.

The mere implication of God as Spirit implies that He is not limited to time and space. His Spirit is invasive and unlimited, permeating every age, speaking every tongue, mastering every history and culture, and moving upon every religious system and all creation. Thus the myriad of religions is not a problem for God. He was not caught by surprise at their emergence. He's got the whole world in His hands and has held the world's religions since eternity.

Islam

The reason the two covenants of the Old Testament compete is a function of competing versions of their history. In the book of Genesis, we have the Judeo-Christian version of God's covenants with Abraham. The Qur'an, however, teaches that Ishmael was the child of promise (Sura 19:54; compare Sura 37:83–109 with Genesis 22:1–19), so Muslims believe God's covenant promises were meant for Ishmael's descendants, not Isaac's.

"Muhammad descended from Ishmael, so Muslims seek to lay claim to these covenant promises, namely the land of Palestine. Since Israel's UN-sanctioned return to Palestine in 1948, there has been unceasing hostility between Israel and her Arab neighbors, with major armed conflicts in 1948–49, 1956, 1967, 1973–74, and 1982. That Israel remains today is a miracle in and of itself" ("Origin of Islam—A Quranic Revelation," All About Religion.org).

Muhammad's time on earth was good and even glorious in many ways. However, according to Muslim historians, he was born April 20, 570 and died June 8, 632. Unlike Jesus, he was born of natural parents, died a natural death, and remains dead.

"The Islamic doctrine of God's nature and attributes coincides with the Christian, insofar as he is by both taught to be the Creator of all things in heaven and earth, who rules and preserves all things, without beginning, omnipotent, omniscient, omnipresent, and full of mercy. But it differs in that Jesus is only a prophet and apostle, although his birth is said to be due to a miraculous, divine operation" ("Biography of Mohammed," www.sacklunch. net/biography/M/Mohammed.html).

Orthodox Muslims believe that Jesus' birth was due to a miraculous, divine operation. According to Muslim scholars, the humanity of Muhammad is undisputed. "The Holy Prophet departed from this world on the 28th of Safar, 11 A.H. Thus ended the life of the Final Prophet sent.

The Islamic prophet Muhammad is buried in the Al-Masjid al-Nabawi (Mosque of the Prophet) in the city of Medina in Saudi Arabia. No extraordinary claims are made for him, the most revered and the last prophet of his founding predecessors." ("Death and Burial," http://www.al islam.org/lifeprophet/24.htm).

What is said of the Muslims relative to the life, death, and burial of their leader can be said of the founders of every other non-Christian religion both major and minor: their founders all are dead.

Hinduism

Hinduism, the oldest of all religions, predates Judaism by eleven hundred years and Christianity by as much as two thousand years if the very oldest pre-Hindu Vedic manuscripts are used. Hinduism is pantheistic because of the belief that God and the material world are one and the same and that God is present in everything. This is a notion shared to some extent by the Judeo-Christian belief that God is omnipresent.

Hinduism is also *polytheistic*, meaning it believes the divine essence, or *Brahman*, manifests or expresses itself in the physical world in the form of physical beings that possess personality. As such, deity is manifested in many gods of many forms. More specifically, Hinduism recognizes three supreme gods: (1) Brahma, the creator; (2) Vishnu, the preserver; and (3) Siva, the destroyer.

Some compare Brahma to God the Father, Vishnu to Jesus, and Siva to the Holy Spirit. In Hinduism, Brahma, Vishnu, and Siva are generally recognized as equal, though certain sects emphasize one or the other. They differ, however, in realms of power and authority. This belief is similar to the Christian doctrine of the Trinity—one God with three manifestations: God the Father, God the Son, and God the Holy Spirit; or said another way, God the creator; God the *logos,* or word; and God the power, or *dunamis.*

Hinduism teaches that God is ultimately an impersonal, eternal force, essence, or power of existence, having none of the attributes of persons, such as knowing, thinking, loving, etc. This force, called Brahman, is present everywhere and in everything in nature, but especially in all living things—every plant, every animal, and especially every human being.

Hinduism teaches that this impersonal essence pervading all things is also found within us. Therefore, the spirit within us is divine; it is part of God. The real inner person is God, and that inner essence is the essence of deity. The *Bhagavad-Gita* says our eternal souls are part and parcel of God. Consequently, the Hindu gods are represented by various statues, images, and icons, but have no material existence or interaction with the believers.

When we understand such concepts, we begin to notice common references. For example, the Force in the Star Wars movies is essentially Brahman, the impersonal universal force present in everywhere and in everything. These concepts have also been popularized by the New Age movement.

The avatars of Hinduism are incarnations of gods who have come to earth as men. The best known are the avatars of Vishnu: (1) Rama and (2) Krishna in the *Bhagavad-Gita*. There are also many lesser deities with various levels or realms of authority. Some rule over certain areas of the earth or certain aspects of nature, such as fire, sun, wealth, water, etc.

Along with these deities, religious teachers and dead ancestors are also worshiped. This worship is popular among the people and often involves the use of many images. The concept of the all-pervading Brahman is mainly theoretical among the religious leaders ("Hinduism: An Overview," *Hinduism Today*, September 2011).

Regardless of what we think of Hinduism as a religion, we are forced to recognize that the search for God is ancient and intense, especially among East Indians. We also note a commonality of expression that is found in most of the larger religions, such as describing God as a "force" or "the force," "the power," or "the presence." Whether God is the force or the force is God, we are required to deal with principles and concepts that appear to have a common thread.

Bahá'í Faith

Located in Bahji near Acre, Israel, the Shrine of Bahá'u'lláh is the holiest place for Bahá'ís and is their *Qiblih*, or direction of prayer. It contains the remains of Bahá'u'lláh, founder of the Bahá'í faith, and is located near the spot where he died in the Mansion of Bahji. Bahá'u'lláh died May 29, 1892, and remains dead.

The Shrine of the Báb, the burial location of the Báb, whom Bahá'ís view as the immediate forerunner of their religion, is located on Mount Carmel in Haifa, Israel. ("Bahai Faith: Baha'U'llah," Wikipedia).

Buddhism

The Buddha's body was cremated, and the relics were placed in monuments, or *stupas*, some of which are believed to have survived until the present. For example, the Temple of the Tooth, or Dalada Maligawa, in Sri Lanka is the place where the right tooth relic of Buddha is kept at present. The Buddha remains dead.

Confucius

> K'ung Fu Tzu (aka Kông Fūzî, K'ung-tze, K'ung-fu-tze, and commonly written as Confucius in English) was born in 551 BC in the state of Lu (modern-day Shantung Province in China). He lived during the Chou dynasty, an era known for its moral laxity. When he was 22 years of age, he opened a school. Success in teaching led to his appointment as minister of justice of Lu. After a conflict with the Marquis of Lu, he left the state and wandered for 13 years throughout China, giving advice to their rulers. He accumulated a small band of students during this time. The last years of his life were spent back in Lu, where he devoted himself to teaching. He died about 479 BC at the approximate age of 72.
>
> His lifetime almost exactly coincided with that of Buddha, who died two years earlier at the age of eighty. His writings deal primarily with individual morality and ethics, and the proper exercise of political power by the rulers. ("Confucianism," *New Advent— Catholic Encyclopedia*, at http://www.newadvent.org/)

The grave of Confucius is located in his hometown of Qufu in Shandong province in a large cemetery where more than one hundred thousand of his descendants are also buried. Confucius and all his descendants are dead and buried—all died and remain dead to this very day. The vast majority of Chinese do not believe or worship him. Perhaps that is due to the fact that Confucianism is more a philosophical moral discipline and K'ung Fu Tzu never intended to start a religion.

I believe the followers of Confucius, Buddha, Bahá'u'lláh, Vishnu, Muhammad, and every other religious or spiritual leader and founder are responding to that siren call embedded in their souls when God created them in His own image as Yahweh Elohim, the Creator God. I also believe that their Father (aka Jehovah God) had them on His mind and so loved them that He died for them and included them in His will. Some, of course, do not know they are in the will and would miss their inheritance if the will bequeathed money, possessions, or property. But the will grants privilege and status redeemable upon the death of the benefactor; therefore, whether they know about it or not, they receive their inheritance along with everyone else.

The Bible says, "My people are destroyed from lack of knowledge" (Hosea 4:6); and "Therefore my people will go into exile for lack of understanding; their men of rank will die of hunger and their masses will be parched with thirst" (Isaiah 5:13). The quality of life on this earth is in direct proportion to the receiving of knowledge. In other words, the more knowledge of God, the benefits left in His will (Old and New Testaments), and the saving grace of His Savior, the better the quality of life in the time realm. Some benefits are immediate and inherited during our lifetime on the earth, and some benefits are long-term and inherited only at the end of time - in eternity.

It is interesting to me that the world's major religions share common beginnings. The story of Noah is honored and shared by Judaism, Christianity, Islam, and the Ba'hai. Even more interesting is that the world's major religions will also share common endings because of the finished work of one Jesus, the Christ.

Our job as Christians, the new Jews (Romans 3:28), the chosen remnant of the New Testament, is to help others navigate the religious twists and turns and lead them to the Father they're really looking for. The inescapable fact remains, their understanding notwithstanding, when God died on the cross (God was in Christ), everyone was justified and everyone's sins were covered—even the sins of foreign sheep from other folds. I find that thought so relieving. No longer do I have to save this crazy world with my denominational perspective or yours. God already has. God is good.

Again, I don't know how He does it or how He will do it; neither do any of the religious pundits know. But I believe His Word, and His Word says clearly, "God so loved the world, that he gave his only begotten Son, that whosoever believeth in him should not perish, but have everlasting life" (John 3:16 KJV). I do not believe that anyone knows who all the "whosoevers" are. Most importantly, I believe that most of humanity scrambles to believe in Him in whatever manner He has revealed Himself, and I don't doubt that He will reveal and save to His own satisfaction, because He said He would.

Could it be that those souls caught up in cultures and communities that are non-Christian by name are the ones Jesus was speaking of when He said in John 10:16, "I have other sheep, too, that are not in this sheepfold. I must bring them also. They will listen to my voice, and there will be one flock with one shepherd" (NLT)? And when these other sheep are brought in, could it be they will not be called Christians, though they will be believers?

Could God be so good that He would really mean what He says in Hebrews 2:9: "What we do see is Jesus, who was given a position 'a little lower than the angels'; and because he suffered death for us, he is now 'crowned with glory and honor.' Yes, by God's grace, Jesus tasted death for everyone" (NLT). Could *everyone* mean… "everyone"? The renowned Albert Barnes seems to think so. He writes:

> How could words affirm more clearly that the atonement made by the Lord Jesus was unlimited in its nature and design? How can we express that idea in more clear or intelligible language? That this refers to the atonement is evident—for it says that he "tasted death" for them. (Albert Barnes, *Barnes' Notes on the New Testament.* Grand Rapids: Kregel Publications, 1966)

Jesus

As for Jesus, Ye'shua, Joshua, meaning "God saves," He was prophesied to come millennia before His immaculate conception and birth, His sinless life, and His crucifixion and death witnessed by thousands. His conspicuous burial and His powerful resurrection are the most unique and powerful claims in the history of religion and humankind. In his article "7 Proofs of the Resurrection," written for About.com Christianity, Jack Zavada writes:

> Archaeological discoveries continue to support the Bible's historical accuracy. We tend to forget that the Gospels and book of Acts are eyewitness accounts of the life and death of Jesus. Further nonbiblical evidence for Jesus' existence comes from the writings of Flavius Josephus, Cornelius Tacitus, Lucian of Samosata, and the Jewish Sanhedrin… The empty tomb may be the strongest proof Jesus Christ rose from

the dead. Two major theories have been advanced by unbelievers: someone stole Jesus' body or the women and disciples went to the wrong tomb. The Jews and Romans had no motive to steal the body. Christ's apostles were too cowardly and would have had to overcome the Roman guards. The women who found the tomb empty had earlier watched Jesus being laid away; they knew where the correct tomb was. Even if they had gone to the wrong tomb, the Sanhedrin could have produced the body from the right tomb to stop the resurrection stories. Jesus' burial cloths were left neatly folded inside, hardly the act of hurrying grave robbers. Angels said Jesus had risen from the dead.

The tomb where they laid Jesus is empty to this day. After His death and burial, more than five hundred people at one time witnessed His appearance, as did also the women at the grave, the two men who walked with Him on the Emmaus road, and His disciples, including one called doubting Thomas.

Jack Zavada's article continues:

Smaller groups also saw the risen Christ, such as the apostles, and Cleopas and his companion. They all saw the same thing, and in the case of the apostles, they touched Jesus and watched him eat food. The hallucination theory is further debunked because after the ascension of Jesus into heaven, sightings of him stopped.

Absolutely no other religion, religious leader, or iconic potentate makes the claim of the Jesus of Christianity. He is alive.

Redemptive Analogies

Nothing illustrates the universal nature of God's intent in clear secular terms like the experience of Don Richardson, missionary to New Guinea, who has written one of the most fascinating books I have ever read, *Eternity in Their Hearts* (Regal Books, revised 1984). The thesis of his writings argues that hidden among tribal cultures are practices or understandings, which he calls "redemptive analogies," that can be used to illustrate the meaning of the Christian gospel and contextualize the biblical representation of the incarnation of Jesus.

In 1962, Richardson and his wife, Carol, and their seven-month-old baby went to work among the Sawi tribe of what was then Dutch New Guinea. The Sawi were known to be cannibalistic headhunters. In their new home in the jungle, the Richardsons set about learning the native Sawi language, which was daunting in its complexity. Though there are nineteen tenses for every verb, Richardson soon became proficient in the dialect.

Richardson labored to use the Bible to show the villagers a way to comprehend Jesus, but the cultural barriers to understanding and accepting his teaching seemed impossible. Then, an unlikely event brought the concept of the substitutionary atonement of Christ into immediate relevance for the Sawi. Missionary historian Ruth A. Tucker writes about it:

> As he learned the language and lived with the people, he became more aware of the gulf that separated his Christian worldview from the worldview of the Sawi: "In their eyes, Judas, not Jesus, was the hero of the Gospels. Jesus was just the dupe to be laughed at." Eventually Richardson discovered what he referred to as a redemptive analogy that pointed to the incarnate Christ far more clearly than any biblical passage alone

could have done. What he discovered was the Sawi concept of the peace child.

The Peace Child

> Three tribal villages were in constant battle at this time. The Richardsons were considering leaving the area, so to keep them there, the Sawi people in the embattled villages came together and decided that they would make peace with their hated enemies. Ceremonies commenced that saw young children being exchanged between opposing villages. One man in particular ran toward his enemy's camp and literally gave his son to his hated foe. Observing this, Richardson wrote: "If a man would actually give his own son to his enemies, that man could be trusted!" From this rare picture came the analogy of God's sacrifice of His own Son. The Sawi began to understand the teaching of the incarnation of Christ in the Gospel after Richardson explained God to them in this way.
>
> Following this event many villagers converted to Christianity, a translation of the New Testament in Sawi was published, and nearly 2500 Sawi patients were treated by Carol. The world's largest circular building made strictly from unmilled poles was constructed in 1972 as a Christian meeting place by the Sawi. (Wikipedia online)

The overwhelming conclusion of Don Richardson's discoveries with more than twenty-five different cultures is that the God of Abraham, Isaac, and Jacob is known in name and concept among many ancient nations, cultures, and languages. The peace child ritual of an ancient people demonstrates a spiritual migration of the knowledge of God to what I call "non-believing believers."

As Ecclesiastes 3:11 says, "He has made everything beautiful in its time. He has also set eternity in the hearts of men." Indeed, there is a calling from eternity that reaches the hearts and souls of people in all the cultures and nations of the world.

It is utterly fascinating to me that so intent was Jesus to establish the inclusive kingdom of God that He never claimed a title or called himself a Christian. Nor did He come to earth in order to establish Christianity. The Bible says He "made himself of no reputation, and took upon him the form of a servant, and was made in the likeness of men" (Philipians 2:7 KJV). He came to earth to establish the kingdom of God, a kingdom that the biblical prophet Daniel prophesied would not come from man and would not be left to man (Daniel 2:44), a kingdom that the prophet Micah said all nations would flow into. Jesus claimed and proved to be God incarnate, God in the flesh, and built the foundation for that kingdom and launched it on the day of Pentecost with a powerful display of universality:

> So when they met together, they asked him, "Lord, are you at this time going to restore the kingdom to Israel?" He said to them: "It is not for you to know the times or dates the Father has set by his own authority. But you will receive power when the Holy Spirit comes on you; and you will be my witnesses in Jerusalem, and in all Judea and Samaria, and to the ends of the earth.
>
> —Acts 1:6–8 (NIV)

The plan was always worldwide. Not only is this powerfully compelling and perhaps indicative of the dynamic spiritual influence of God through Jesus, but it also reflects the fulfilling of both the Abrahamic covenant and the covenant with Hagar and Ishmael found in Genesis 21:8–21.

The world God so loved has access to Him through Jesus and because of Jesus. Jesus was God's gift to the world—all of the world's religious confusion notwithstanding. His work at Calvary was twofold: (1) the remission of sin and (2) the reconciliation of God with all humankind. In addition, 2 Corinthians 5:19 says, "For God was in Christ, reconciling the world to himself, no longer counting people's sins against them. And he gave us this wonderful message of reconciliation" (NLT). In every way and in every place, God, at least in principle has saved everybody in the world and He does it by the free gift of grace through faith. (Ephesians 2:8)

Another thing happened at Calvary that emphasizes the universal nature of the kingdom of God: "At that moment the curtain of the temple was torn in two from top to bottom; the earth shook and the rocks split" (Matthew 27:51). It was precisely at this point that Genesis 3:15 was fulfilled: "it shall bruise thy head, and thou shalt bruise his heel" (KJV). Symbolically and comparatively, the crucifixion only bruised Jesus' heel, but His death and resurrection reunited God and man forever, symbolically crushing Satan's head. If the benefit of Jesus' death and resurrection was only temporary, then Satan's wound would not have been mortal. But if the benefit was permanent, then Satan was dealt a blow that was fatal and forever, his dominion and power virtually broken. The first messianic prophecy was fulfilled in the last act of God on the cross. The problem of sin was solved. For all intents and purposes, we are now playing out the clock as agents and ambassadors sharing the Good News of reconciliation.

The division between man and man was only the collateral damage caused by the division between God and man. The division between God and man was the central problem, and the reconciliation between God and man was central to God's plan of salvation. When Adam and Eve sinned by disobeying God in the Garden of Eden, they brought instant division between God, themselves, and all humanity. Man became unplugged from his source and began to die.

God, however, immediately launched the plan whose purpose was the reconciliation of God and man, not God and religion. Religion is merely an extension of man's sin. Religion about God as opposed to relationship with God became man's fig-leaf attempt at restoration. Religion was to the fig leaf as faith was to the animal-skin covering God used in Genesis 3:21. Man could not cover himself then, and he cannot cover himself now. Thank God for the blood!

The Great Divide

Let's talk about the broken-down wall of partition and the torn curtain in a little more detail. From the Garden of Eden to Calvary, a wall existed between God and man, symbolized by the actual wall restricting the Gentiles to the outer court of the temple.

According to the *International Standard Bible Encyclopedia*, a century ago excavations at the temple site unearthed portions of this wall and discovered this inscription: "No man of another nation is to enter within the fence and enclosure round the Temple. Whoever is caught will have himself to blame that his death ensues."

The Apostle Paul was all too familiar with this division, and was accused of violating its sacred tradition in Acts 21:28–30. Luke records that when the Jews saw Paul in their temple, they

> laid hands on him, crying out, Men of Israel, help us.
> This is the man, that teacheth all men every where

against the people, and the law, and this place: and
he further brought Greeks also into the temple, and
hath polluted this holy place. (For they had seen
before with him in the city Trophimus an Ephesian,
whom they supposed that Paul had brought into the
temple.) And all the city was moved, and the people
ran together: and they took Paul, and drew him out of
the temple: and forthwith the doors were shut. (KJV)

So, the symbol of separation between God and man was
expanded by religion to be the segregation of Jew and Gentile; but
the tearing of the temple veil and the destruction of the middle
wall in the outer court of the temple were dramatic symbols of
God's intent to remove all man-made religious division. "For he is
our peace, who hath made both one, and hath broken down the
middle wall of partition between us" (Ephesians 2:14).

No longer is there a distinction between priest and people,
or between Jew and Gentile, or any other difference. "There
is neither Greek nor Jew, circumcision nor uncircumcision,
Barbarian, Scythian, bond nor free: but Christ is all, and in all"
(Colossians 3:11).

However, by the time the wall of partition was destroyed at
Calvary, humankind had sought cover behind a new "fig leaf"—
religion—which only served to divide them from each other.
Consequently, the apostle Paul announced in 2 Corinthians
5:16–22:

No longer, then, do we judge anyone by human
standards. Even if at one time we judged Christ
according to human standards, we no longer do so.
Anyone who is joined to Christ is a new being; the old
is gone, the new has come. All this is done by God,
who through Christ changed us from enemies into
his friends and gave us the task of making others his

friends also. Our message is that God was making the whole human race his friends through Christ. God did not keep an account of their sins, and he has given us the message which tells how he makes them his friends. Here we are, then, speaking for Christ, as though God himself were making his appeal through us. We plead on Christ's behalf: let God change you from enemies into his friends! Christ was without sin, but for our sake God made him share our sin in order that in union with him we might share the righteousness of God. (GNT)

Righteous by mere association? Could God be this good?

The New Jew and New Gentile

With the veil torn and the wall removed, separation of man and God and the segregation of Jews (the "chosen") from Gentiles (everybody else) is eliminated. This represents a major paradigm shift. The death and resurrection of God through Christ not only saved the world that He loved but also removed all religious and racial distinctions. "There is [now no distinction] neither Jew nor Greek, there is neither slave nor free, there is not male and female; for you are all one in Christ Jesus." (Galatians 3:28 AMP) Then the apostle Paul, himself a Jew, redefines who is Jewish:

> For he is not a Jew, which is one outwardly; neither is that circumcision, which is outward in the flesh: But he is a Jew, which is one inwardly; and circumcision is that of the heart, in the spirit, and not in the letter; whose praise is not of men, but of God
> (ROMANS 2:28–29 KJV).

Could it be that the physical Jew of the Old Testament was the type and shadow of the New Testament believer? And could it be that the physical Gentile of the Old Testament is the mixed multitude of religions from the New Testament forward? Because of the destruction of the middle wall of partition that separated believing Gentiles from natural-born Jews in the courtyard of the Herodian temple, we all have been granted access to God. By the tearing of the veil in the temple, we have access, not only to the court of the temple, but all the way to the Holy of Holies.

When Jesus died, the veil was torn from top to bottom, signifying two very important things: (1) there was now equal access to God, and (2) the tearing from top to bottom was done by the hand of God. The tearing of the veil meant that both Jew and Gentile could come directly into the presence of God, "for there is only one God and one Mediator who can reconcile God and humanity—the man Christ Jesus" (1 Timothy 2:5 NLT). Please note that the mediating work has been done. The work that causes man to be reconciled is done.

Would it follow, then, that New Testament Gentiles (believers in other folds) are those who are not traditionally viewed as natural born, or born-again Christians, but who are nonetheless believers who are the sheep of another fold? Could Jesus be angry that the modern-day Gentiles are banished to an outer court of His kingdom because we born-again Christians tend not to recognize them? Certainly that is so. Are the believers that Jesus says He will bring into the sheepfold being asked for proof of birth by modern-day Christian "birthers"? How repulsive. Like the Old Testament Gentiles barred from entering the temple because of their place of birth, they are being disqualified from seeking after God because of dissimilar revelation.

At a confrontation in the Herodian temple, Jesus shed light on this topic when He cited Isaiah 56, which says the following in its larger context in verses 1–8:

> Thus says the LORD: "Keep justice, and do righteousness, for soon my salvation will come, and my deliverance be revealed. Blessed is the man who does this, and the son of man who holds it fast, who keeps the Sabbath, not profaning it, and keeps his hand from doing any evil."
>
> Let not the foreigner who has joined himself to the LORD say, "The LORD will surely separate me from his people"; and let not the eunuch say, "Behold, I am a dry tree." For thus says the LORD: "To the eunuchs who keep my Sabbaths, who choose the things that please me and hold fast my covenant, I will give in my house and within my walls a monument and a name better than sons and daughters; I will give them an everlasting name that shall not be cut off.
>
> "And the foreigners who join themselves to the LORD, to minister to him, to love the name of the LORD, and to be his servants, everyone who keeps the Sabbath and does not profane it, and holds fast my covenant—these I will bring to my holy mountain, and make them joyful in my house of prayer; their burnt offerings and their sacrifices will be accepted on my altar; for my house shall be called a house of prayer for all peoples."
>
> The Lord GOD, who gathers the outcasts of Israel, declares, "I will gather yet others to him besides those already gathered." (ESV)

It took the removal of the middle wall of partition and the tearing of the veil in the temple to bring these others into the one fold. I repeat, Jesus said, "I have other sheep, too, that are not in this sheepfold. I must bring them also. They will listen to my voice, and there will be one flock with one shepherd" (John 10:16 NLT).

He did "bring them also" when He shouted triumphantly from the cross, "It is finished!" The wall was torn down. God Himself ripped the veil in the temple that separated Him from us, us from Him, and us from each other. Sin separated us, but not anymore. *It is finished!* Sin produced all manner of separation, segregation, discrimination, alienation, and isolation, but not anymore. *It is finished!* Sin divided us by race, religion, color, gender, language, culture, nationality, and economic status, but not anymore. *It is finished!* Creation has been saved by the suffering act of God's love. He's that good, I tell you! *God is that good!*

CHAPTER 6

PAID FORWARD

But God commendeth his love toward us, in that, while we were yet sinners, Christ died for us.
—ROMANS 5:8 (KJV)

There is a real good-news story that religion (human beliefs and opinions concerning God) doesn't want you to know. It is a truth so powerful it reveals many of our religious rituals, practices, and beliefs as over the top, as some of them really are. Those who discover this truth are set free from the bondage of man worship and man rule. Here it is: the best news you have ever heard in your life is that Jesus paid the penalty for all the sins of everybody in the world, past, present, and future. BAM!—there it is—end of story. Now let's worship the God who is *that* good!

As Adam's sin of disobedience cursed, corrupted, and contaminated forward to unborn generations and to all people of the earth (for we are born in sin and shaped in iniquity, according to Psalm 51:5), so also does the obedience and sacrificial death of Jesus Christ, the second Adam, pay the debt forward to unborn generations and all people of the earth. According to

2 Corinthians 5:20, not only are our sins commuted forward, but also His righteousness is applied forward to us, and in the process, all humanity wins in principle and most of humanity wins in practice.

Unless we deliberately and with great premeditation crawl out from under such a wonderful covering, we win—we are saved. Being lost or condemned to eternal punishment, whatever that may be, is all but impossible. It is God who has made the arrangement to save us all. Thus God's covenant with Abraham is fulfilled by Jesus' death on the cross.

God said to Abraham, "All peoples on earth will be blessed through you." Don't miss that word *all*. All means all. The sovereign, omnipotent, and omniscient God intended and arranged for all to be blessed. Now go tell it on the mountain! God's love separates Him from all competitors by its depth, height, breadth, and width. He outperforms our imagination. He over-performs our expectation.

Again, when Jesus died on the cross, He paid for my sins in advance, although I wasn't born until approximately two thousand years later. By the time I opened my mouth to utter something foul, rebellious, and self-righteous, the blood of Jesus had already been shed and was covering me from the moment of my first acceptance of his free grace through his free faith. When I committed acts of rank and outright sin, an act of God had already forgiven me, and the power of God had already lined me up to meet His love that would change me and continue a good work in me until the day of Jesus Christ (Philippians 1:6).

Think about it. According to "The Chronology of Jesus' Crucifixion" by Dr. Ralph F. Wilson, Jesus was crucified on the cross in April of 33 AD, which was 1,980 years ago. Since I was born in 1945 that was 1,912 years before I was even born. All my many sins—big and small, known and unknown—were in the future when my Savior died on the cross.

Planned In Eternity

As great as the Christmas story is, there is an even greater story that precedes it: the story of God being in Christ. After Adam's fall, the plan for man's ultimate salvation and reconciliation with God was not an afterthought. It was planned before the foundation of the world. John the Baptist saw Jesus and exclaimed, "Behold! The Lamb of God who takes away the sin of the world!" (John 1:29 NKJV). This announcement heralded the beginning of the end of Satan's dominion and announced the arrival of the redemption of humankind all over the world and throughout all ages. However, you must not miss the premeditation of Jesus' blood sacrifice.

1 Peter 1:19-20 (NASB) is stunning in its implications:

> but with precious blood, as of a lamb unblemished and spotless, *the blood* of Christ. For He was foreknown before the foundation of the world, but has appeared in these last times for the sake of you...

"Foreknown before the foundation of the world" suggests the total premeditation of God's plan to save His creation. The blood of Christ foreknown before the foundation of the world covered the very first sin ever committed and covers the very last sin ever to be committed. The plan was not left to chance and was not subject to the vicissitudes of worldly events. God came down Himself to save us and no demon in hell could stop Him or top Him. Like the story of the "Good Samaritan" He paid for my present need and my future need.

The remedy for sin preceded the acts of sin. The remedy for sin was in place before the earth was formed. God anticipated man's abuse of freewill so He put in place the perfect sacrifice that would "take away the sins of the world" – Himself. God's plan to pay for man's sin began in eternity – that's as advanced as it gets - and was completed with the triumphant announcement "It is finished" at Calvary. There is nothing left to do to effect humankind's justification. The only thing humankind can do is – accept the gift. It is important to remember you are not justified because you repented; you repented because you are justified. "The goodness of God leads men to repentance." (Romans 2:4) The God ordained penalty for Adam's sin was death. Justice required the guilty to die. God through Jesus stepped in and died on behalf of the guilty. The penalty was satisfied. At the moment of the death of the Lamb of God the guilty were justified. Repentance was not the payment for justification – death was the payment.

What I'm about to say next may be the most important part of the whole story of salvation: At the moment of Jesus' final words, all humankind everywhere past, present and future was covered by His blood. Justification happened to the guilty. The guilty could do nothing to obtain it. This is why it is so important to understand that it was the eternal timeless God on the cross in person of Jesus Christ. Jesus' death justified us and Jesus' resurrection converts us or brought new life. The process of full salvation begins with justification – the payment of the penalty for sin. His acts are as eternal as His person. His love is an eternal for-all-time love. His forgiveness was and is an eternal for-all-time forgiveness. His blood is eternal and covers sin from the beginning of time to the end of time. His grace reaches the past sinners who didn't have all the post-Calvary knowledge; the present sins of the soldiers at the foot of the cross who acknowledged him saying,

"Surely this man was the Son of God" and his grace reached you and me over 2000 years into the future.

It is important that we continue forward in our thinking and understand why Genesis 3:15 is called the first messianic prophecy. This important verse of Scripture reads:

> And I will put enmity between thee and the woman and between thy seed and her seed; it shall bruise thy head, and thou shalt bruise his heel. (KJV)

At the time of this prophecy, the fulfillment of this bruising was at least six thousand years in the future, according to J. Howlett ("Biblical Chronology" in the *Catholic Encyclopedia*, New York: Robert Appleton Company, 1908). The soldier's spear in the side of Jesus was the last "bruise," and it was the finishing act of payment for sin and the first act of justification for all humankind. As Isaiah prophesied, Jesus was "wounded for our transgressions, he was bruised for our iniquities: the chastisement of our peace was upon him; and with his stripes we are healed [delivered]" (Isa. 53:5 KJV).

The blood and water that rushed from His side were prophetic prerequisite symbols of man's redemption and reconciliation. The blood symbolized the covering for sin: "In fact, the law requires that nearly everything be cleansed with blood, and without the shedding of blood there is no forgiveness" (Hebrews 9:22). By the shedding of Jesus' blood, justice was satisfied at that moment. At the moment of Jesus' death the penalty was paid.

The water symbolized the unleashed power of God that had incubated in the Savior for thirty-three years. The soldier's spear unleashed the Creator's power; the same power that created the world was now available to all who would believe, thus fulfilling John 12:24:

> I tell you the truth, unless a kernel of wheat falls to the
> ground and dies, it remains only a single seed. But if
> it dies, it produces many seeds.

The seed fell to the ground and died, and true to the
prophecy, it produced the day of Pentecost. On that birth day of
the kingdom of God on earth, three thousand souls were added,
and signs and wonders highlighted the new paradigm. The death
of Jesus and the life-giving acts of the Holy Spirit went on to
produce many seeds. Satan's head was, and is still being, crushed.
He was powerless against the Spirit-filled New Testament church
and is no match for the universal Spirit-empowered kingdom of
God of this day.

Satan's fate was predestined. Jesus' victory over sin and Satan
was prophesied. The scope of the ultimate victory had to be
comparable to the scope of the initial defeat in the Garden of
Eden. It is documented throughout Scripture, beginning with
Genesis 3:15 and including Isaiah 43 and Matthew 1:21.

Romans 5:17 is the classic scripture that tells us just how good
God is:

> For the sin of this one man, Adam, caused death to
> rule over many. But even greater is God's wonderful
> grace and his gift of righteousness, for all who receive
> it will live in triumph over sin and death through this
> one man, Jesus Christ. (NLT)

We must celebrate the victory won for us at the cross and
know that the enemy of our souls was defeated, is defeated, and
will be defeated. The Bible says the way God saved us is a measure
of His love for us in that He commended His love toward us while
we were yet sinners (Romans 5:8). That is to say, our sins were
forgiven before they were ever committed. We are redeemed and

will be redeemed, and we can no longer be separated from God's love. As the hymn writer so eloquently says, "Jesus paid it all, / All to Him I owe; / Sin had left a crimson stain, / He washed it white as snow."

Paid Forward

Just then a religion scholar stood up with a question to test Jesus. "Teacher, what do I need to do to get eternal life?"

He answered, "What's written in God's Law? How do you interpret it?"

He said, "That you love the Lord your God with all your passion and prayer and muscle and intelligence—and that you love your neighbor as well as you do yourself." "Good answer!" said Jesus. "Do it and you'll live."

Looking for a loophole, he asked, "And just how would you define 'neighbor'?"

Jesus answered by telling a story. "There was once a man traveling from Jerusalem to Jericho. On the way he was attacked by robbers. They took his clothes, beat him up, and went off leaving him half-dead. Luckily, a priest was on his way down the same road, but when he saw him he angled across to the other side. Then a Levite religious man showed up; he also avoided the injured man.

"A Samaritan traveling the road came on him. When he saw the man's condition, his heart went out to him. He gave him first aid, disinfecting and bandaging his wounds. Then he lifted him onto his donkey, led him to an inn, and made him comfortable. In the morning he took out two silver coins and gave them to the innkeeper, saying, 'Take good care of him. If it costs any more, put it on my bill—I'll pay you on my way back.'

"What do you think? Which of the three became a neighbor to the man attacked by robbers?"

"The one who treated him kindly," the religion scholar responded.

Jesus said, "Go and do the same."

—LUKE 10:25–37 (MSG)

We must understand the history of the Samaritans and the Jews to properly appreciate this story. The short version of their history is that certain Jews were considered purebred Jews, while the Samaritans, who did not recognize Jerusalem as the holy capital of the Jewish religion and had intermarried with heathen Gentiles, were considered half-breeds and "dogs" by other Jews (see Luke 9 and John 4).

A brilliant article written by the master teacher Bob Deffinbaugh, ThM, and entitled "The Good Samaritan" summarizes the significance of the differences between the Jewish priest and Levite, and the Samaritan:

> What is Jesus trying to teach this Jewish lawyer here, by telling him this story? Overall, I believe that Jesus is attempting to show this lawyer that the Jewish religious system of that day was completely bankrupt. The lawyer thought of Judaism as owning the only franchise offering tickets to the "kingdom of God," and anyone who did not obtain their official approval as imposters.

The lesson learned in Jesus' parable is threefold:

1. The Samaritan did not have the "right" belief system, yet the system he had was worthy of eternal life.

2. Not only did the Good Samaritan pay for the injured man's immediate needs, but he also paid for his future needs. He paid it forward.
3. Doing the right thing trumps being in the right religion or having the right belief system.

Tell me, who does something like that? Who arranges to pay for the care of an injured stranger—in advance? Jesus, the consummate Good Samaritan, does. Can God be this good?

CHAPTER 7

HE WILL SAVE

And she shall bring forth a son, and thou shalt call his name JESUS: for he shall save his people from their sins.
—MATTHEW 1:21 (KJV)

The Only Way You Can Go to Hell

Early in my first pastorate, at around the age of twenty-seven, I said these dramatic words in the passion of preaching about the power of the gospel: "The only way you can go to hell is to work at it." From that bright Sunday morning at the Sumpter Community Church of God, I broke with tradition and began to preach a gospel that was truly *gospel*, or "Good News." Today, many years removed from that dramatic announcement, my theology and I have evolved into certainty. I am absolutely sure that God wins the battle between good and evil, and as a result, we win too. We are His children, and He *will* save.

Here Are the Problems

In the slightly delusional world of religion and religious extremes, a gamut of choices exists between faith and feeling, make-believe and miracle, saint and sinner, Christ and crazy. The options are laid out like choices in a religious smorgasbord. You and I, whether simple or sound, must choose this day whom, what, where, and if we will serve God, Allah, Vishnu, or some other higher being proposed by whomever. Do we seriously believe that the burden of making the right choice is our burden alone? Is there a higher being somewhere having fun messing with our heads as we spin in chaos and confusion, trying to figure out how not to go to a hell, a place where we will burn forever and ever? Or does it make more sense that Jehovah Elohim, the Creator of us all, has fixed it so that *whosoever will* - will believe sufficiently to be saved?

A second problem arises out of the more fundamental question, do we find God or does God find us? Does God create us and then throw us into the middle of the mess of this world and say, "Now find Me or else"? Or does He create us with a programmed destiny to finish as winners and as souls imprinted with an image that responds to His call from home, which is in eternity. And could it be, even if we are deaf-mutes or mentally ill, somehow we respond, and no matter how feeble or misguided our response, He hears our faintest cry from wherever we are on earth and restores us?

A third problem deals with the concept of eternity and is entirely one of perspective. We try to stuff eternity inside of time, and, of course, it doesn't fit. Eternity holds all the secrets that manifest as puzzles, paradoxes, and parallel truths in the time realm. Our problem is to keep them sorted and comprehend their impact on our understanding of the Word, and to arrive at livable conclusions.

For instance, I will never understand how eighty to a hundred years of sin is equal to a billion years in the lake of fire, or hell. How could anything done in time justify punishment throughout eternity, unless these are hyperbolic values that illustrate the severity of consequences for all evil not covered by the blood of Jesus? I can accept someone going to hell, just not for forever. I mean, come on, does it seem right for a person to spend eternity in everlasting fire and burning pain for something that took five minutes in time? Isn't that cruel and unusual punishment on steroids by any standard? With my humanity, as flawed as it is, can I love and embrace with confidence a God I secretly perceive to be unfair, sadistic and vindictive?

So am I to understand eternity in hell as literal or figurative? Yes, God is sovereign. Yes, God can do whatever He wants. But He has said what He wants: that no one should perish, but that all should come to repentance. My argument is that He is as just as He is sovereign. He is as loving as He is just. And He is fair. He died, not for me to spend eternity in hell, but for me to spend eternity in heaven, my original home.

God is not determined to kill me. He is determined to save me. It's really not about hell—it has never been about hell. It has always been about Him and me. He has handled the hell thing. Sometimes I think the emphasis on hell has been the preacher's leverage to make people come to church or pay their tithes.

For the saints, hell is not an option; it is a nonstarter and a non-issue. Death and hell lose their terror in the face of the eternal, all-covering blood of God. God has intervened from the very beginning of time and set up a fail-safe plan of salvation. God gets the last word about the consequences of good and evil, and the last word is what He spoke from the cross for all humankind and for all time and throughout eternity—*"It is finished!"*

Therein lies the balance to the equation of consequences in time and eternity: it is finished. The God of eternity closed the books on time. In eternity, all the books are balanced, and all the accounts are settled. All creation has been forgiven. Even though everything around us in time looks like a never-ending hot mess, the truth is, "now are we the sons of God, and it doth not yet appear what we shall be: but we know that, when he shall appear we shall be like him; for we shall see him as he is" (1 John 3:2 KJV). Indeed, we will then see what He sees. Since the cross, God sees us through rose (or maybe blood) colored glasses.

Maybe someone will go to hell. I just don't know who it is. I don't know who could escape or evade this God kind of love. Who could be that hard and that committed to evil? I sure wouldn't want to meet that person in a dark alley. Remember, redemption is passive. If you do nothing, you win. You don't do anything to earn it. God wills to redeem you. You must actively and, according to Romans 1:21, knowingly reject the deal. God has expressly stated He wills to save and He wills that none should perish. He is not a whimpering, hoping deity. He is not just potent—He is omni - potent. No flask of whiskey; stick of joint; hit of crack; act of adultery; murderous assault; perpetrator or victim of molestation, rape, or violence; crazy religion; or act of insanity (temporary or permanent) is unforgiven and not covered by the blood of God.

So settle it, then: redemption has been accomplished because our God reigns. Neither good religion nor bad religion, neither your understanding nor my understanding or our misunderstanding can defeat the love, will, and goodness of the sovereign God. Problem solved—He will save!

Salvation Is of the Lord

God is a God of order. His order is testimony of His will to save. Nothing He does is accidental. The chaos humankind brought into God's creation by their disobedience did not undo the order in His eternal strategy. From the first day in time, God initiated His universal strategy to have a relationship with His creation. Life on earth may have begun in East Africa, but it was designed in eternity. On earth, we live in the moment, but in eternity, our salvation is a done deal. As Jeremiah 1:5 says, "Before I formed you in the womb I knew you, before you were born I set you apart."(NIV)

God's intention and instruction for the human race to occupy the planet is clear:

> And God blessed them, and God said unto them, Be fruitful and multiply, and replenish the earth, and subdue it: and have dominion over the fish of the sea, and over the fowl of the air, and over every living thing that moveth upon the earth.
>
> —GENESIS 1:28 (KJV)

God's will for His creation is brought to pass by His sovereign omniscience and omnipotence. The mystery of the time realm prevents us from seeing the end from the beginning; however, there are no mysteries in eternity. The time-bound universe in which we live is ordered by universal laws that govern its existence, a universal strategy to guide it, and, most importantly, a universal application to make it all happen.

The laws of the physical universe are constant and function apart from human agreement or belief. Likewise, the laws of the spiritual universe that govern the relationship between man and God are also constant and do not require human agreement or belief. Consequently, a person's physical and spiritual quality of life is in direct proportion to his obedience to his revelation of spiritual law.

For instance, the law of gravity works the same in Chengdu, China, as it does in Walla Walla, Washington, because it is a universal law. You can use mathematical formulas to discover great facts of physics regarding our earth, and no matter where you live on the earth, those laws remain constant. They are universal.

The point is, the same order that created the physical universe is the order that created the strategy for dealing with the spiritual universe. There are laws that govern our relationship with God, the Creator. But for a law to be universal, whether physical or spiritual, it necessarily must work the same; that is, universally. Among the multitude of religious practices, the one constant is God. The differences in religious practices are functions of the variables of language, tradition, information, natural and supernatural events and timing. However, God's principles remain constant.

The Bible is not a book of divine absolutes; it is a book of divine principles. King David, the greatest Jewish King ever; the writer of most of the Psalms; the murderer of one of his best soldiers; the audacious adulterer and the man who in spite of his treachery never stopped being "a man after God's own heart"- never stopped being king. The Holy and all knowing God partners with flawed humankind to accomplish His divine purpose. He seems not to require the letter of perfection but the spirit of principle - "He has made us competent as ministers of a new covenant—not of the letter but of the Spirit; for the letter kills, but the Spirit gives life." (2 Corinthians 3:6)

Our problem as human beings is we lack God's infinite abilities. We think too highly of our lowly finite thoughts. We inadvertently diminish God by our finite and parochial understanding of His infinite person, purpose, and grace and His infinite manifestations and revelations of Himself. He is so awesome that men and women of every nation and tongue possess a theology or philosophy of Him or of His nonexistence.

In the time realm, what man sees as differences and variables has been calculated in eternity and is constant to the omniscient creator God. However, the differences and variables presented by historical event, language, custom, information, and timing produce mystery, speculation, and philosophy in the time realm and prevent humankind from seeing the end from the beginning, as the Creator does.

God determined to save us from before the foundation of the world. He is the omniscient Jehovah, who planned our escape from the penalty of sin and designed the lifestyle we should live in order to maximize our purpose as determined by Him from before the foundation of the world:

> How blessed is God! And what a blessing he is! He's the Father of our Master, Jesus Christ, and takes us to the high places of blessing in him. Long before he laid down earth's foundation, he had us in mind, had settled on us as the focus of his love, to be made whole and holy by his love.
>
> —Ephesians 1:3–4 (MSG)

Furthermore, He created time; He created the world and everything that is:

> In the beginning the Word already existed; the Word was with God. And the Word was God. Through him God made all things; not one thing in all creation was made without him.
>
> —John 1:1–3 (GNT)

Likewise, He says clearly:

> For everything, absolutely everything, above and
> below, visible and invisible, rank after rank after rank
> of angels—everything got started in him and finds its
> purpose in him. He was there before any of it came
> into existence and holds it all together right up to this
> moment.
>
> —Colossians 1:16–17 (MSG)

By the way, if you were the creator, omnipotent and omniscient, would you plan to fail? Would you plan the loss of your creation? Just a thought.

The Bible clearly states it is not God's will "that *any* should perish, but that *all* should come to repentance" (2 Peter 3:9 KJV, emphasis added). God has willed *all* to come to repentance, and the sovereign, all-powerful God always gets His way in the end. The will of God will prevail over the will of man every time. Man's will is no match for God's will-shaping love that brings us to obedience by wooing our "want-to." The love of God is the antidote for the rebellious will of man. Now, let me say again, I believe *all* is a principle. In other words, I believe that God absolutely desires all to come to repentance and that in principle all will. In practice, some will choose not to change (repent).

Take Jonah, for example. In direct disobedience to God's order that he sail to Nineveh and warn the people of impending judgment, he decided instead to sail to Tarshish, in an attempt to flee the presence of the Lord. In response, God did not make Jonah obey; He made him want to obey: "But the Lord sent out a great wind into the sea, and there was a mighty tempest in the sea, so that the ship was like to be broken" (Jonah 1:4 KJV). Jonah was thrown overboard in an effort to save the innocent men on the ship. He was swallowed by a great fish in whose belly he stayed three days and three nights until he began his prayer of deliverance: "I cried by reason of mine affliction unto the Lord, and he heard me; out of the belly of hell cried I, and thou heardest my voice" (Jonah 2:2 KJV). In the midst of this terrorizing experience, Jonah made the statement that sprung him from his prison: "I will pay that that I have vowed. Salvation is of the LORD" (v. 9).

With Jonah's will changed, the Lord now moved. Verse 10 reads, "And the LORD spake unto the fish, and it vomited out Jonah upon the dry land." God did not make Jonah go to Nineveh; He made him willing to go. Jonah was saved because God wanted to save him; God arranged for Jonah to be saved. Nineveh was saved because God wanted to save it. God will save.

For sure, there is no such thing as free will except there be free choice. The first Adam freely chose to disobey God and thereby plunged himself and all of humanity into sin. Likewise, the second Adam, Jesus Christ, freely chose to obey: "And being found in appearance as a man, he humbled himself and became obedient to death—even death on a cross!" (Philippians 2:8). Again it was a predetermined arrangement because "our God is a God who saves; from the Sovereign LORD comes escape from death" (Psalm 68:20).

God was so determined to save us that He did not leave it to a prince, a principality, or a human potentate. He came Himself with both the will and power to save.

Unconditional Love

God also manifests the intensity of His determination to save through the nature of His love. It is unconditional.

Nowhere in the Holy Bible does it say that God loved man on the condition that man love Him back or even that man obey

Him. God went to the cross because He loved us, not because we loved Him. As Jesus said in John 15:16, "Ye have not chosen me, but I have chosen you" (KJV). There was no negotiation. There was no contingency plan based on man's response or reaction. This was about the love of God, and it was unilateral. Romans 5:8 says it clearly: "God commendeth his love toward us, in that, while we were yet, sinners Christ died for us" (KJV).

God's love is unconditional and inseparable. The apostle Paul wrote compellingly of this in Romans 8:

> Can anything separate us from the love of Christ? Can trouble, pain or persecution? Can lack of clothes and food, danger to life and limb, the threat of force of arms? Indeed some of us know the truth of the ancient text: "For your sake we are killed all day long; we are accounted as sheep for the slaughter." No, in all these things we win an overwhelming victory through him who has proved his love for us. I have become absolutely convinced that neither death nor life, neither messenger of Heaven nor monarch of earth, neither what happens today nor what may happen tomorrow, neither a power from on high nor a power from below, nor anything else in God's whole world has any power to separate us from the love of God in Jesus Christ our Lord!
>
> —Romans 8:35–39 (Phillips)

The thief on the cross was saved unconditionally. There were absolutely no formulas or preconditions. He did not go to paradise with Jesus because of his knowledge or his confession and repentance of sin. He had neither. He never asked to be saved, only remembered. Again, the thief did not ask for paradise, but he got it anyway. That's called grace—undeserved favor. He was in a nothing-to-lose condition and responded to *something* in his gut (What could that have been?). No instruction was given and no bargain was struck, yet on that Good Friday, he found favor beyond what he deserved or desired.

William Cowper, recovering from mental illness in the bowels of an insane asylum, penned these unforgettable words:

> There is a fountain filled with blood drawn from Emmanuel's veins,
> And sinners plunged beneath that flood lose all their guilty stain.
> The dying thief rejoiced to see that fountain in his day;
> And there have I, though vile as he, washed all my sins away.

Contrast that with the thief on the other side of Jesus, who chose to rail on Him. This man wanted to live. Unlike the other thief, and perhaps like you and me, his desperation to live numbed his recognition of opportunity. In a matter of minutes the conditions for his sins being forgiven and his debt to both society and God could be paid. Both thieves, the Roman soldiers who were carrying out the crucifixion, and everybody in the world since the world began were about to have their sins forgiven and their sentence of eternal death commuted – by grace. They need only believe – not perform – believe. Out of the three two appear to believe: the soldiers at the cross confessed "Surely, this man was the Son of God" and the believing thief simply said "remember me." By the way, I know this may make some of you crazy, but I will not be surprised if we see both thieves in heaven. It's called – GRACE.

Here it comes—listen up! As Jesus spoke, the heads of the two thieves, throbbing in pain, snapped around in awe at the sound and meaning of Jesus' words: "Father, forgive them, for they know not what they do."

No one had asked Him for this gift of forgiveness. It was not offered as part of a deal—it was freely given. The sins of all humankind would be forgiven, not because they asked, but because He asked and was shedding His holy blood according to the plan made in eternity before the world began; that is, without the shedding of blood, there is no remission for sin. When Jesus requests the Father to forgive them, he gave no condition. It was a sovereign act of love from the Sovereign Lord. There was not a scriptural formula to fulfill or to follow. This was unscripted. Was the request granted? I ask you again – was the request granted. Could God be *that* good?

All humanity made bail that afternoon. At the cross, "Mercy there was great and grace was free / Pardon there was multiplied to me / There my burdened soul found liberty." (William R. Newell) The favor of God's forgiveness was undeserved and unearned. It was God's answer to evil. It was God's greatest act of love. It was the foundation of man's transformation. It was premeditated, arbitrary and deliberate.

In Jesus' announcement of forgiveness and His declaration that the plan was finished and the debt paid, Adam's sin was covered. David's sins were covered, and the sins of Abraham, Isaac, Jacob, and their seed were covered. The sins of the Roman soldiers who administered His crucifixion, the apostle Paul's sins, your sins and my sins (and we weren't even born yet), and the sins of all the generations to come on all seven continents of the world were covered. It was all made possible because of Who was doing the dying. The one act of Adam cast us into sin with all of its consequences, and the one act of God through Jesus reversed the curse and reconciled God and man. (Romans 5:18) Could God be *that* good? Deep down in my Christian Jesus-loving belly, I believe He is just that good.

No Greater Love

There is no greater love than God's unconditional love. His love sets the bar and is the standard. That standard is stated in His Word: "Greater love hath no man than this, that a man lay down his life for his friends" (John 15:13 KJV). And, "I am the good shepherd. The good shepherd lays down his life for the sheep" (John 10:11). "Very rarely will anyone die for a righteous man, though for a good man someone might possibly dare to die. But God demonstrates his own love for us in this: While we were still sinners, Christ died for us" (Romans 5:7–8).

The renowned theologian Albert Barnes once said:

> It greatly enhances the love of Christ, that while the instances of those who have been willing to die for friends have been so rare, he was willing to die for enemies—bitter foes, who rejected his reign, persecuted him, reviled him, scorned him, and sought his life, 1 John 4:10; Romans 5:6; Romans 5:10. It also shows us the extent of his love that he gave himself up, not to common sufferings, but to the most bitter, painful, and protracted sorrows; not for himself, not for friends, but for a thoughtless and unbelieving world. (Albert Barnes, *Notes on the Bible*, Eates and Lauriate, 1834)

Is Dr. Barnes suggesting that the love of God ignores the sin of man or is granted despite the sin of man? (I believe the latter.) Is this why God clearly states, "And thou shalt call his name JESUS: for he *shall* save his people from their sins" (Matthew 1:21 KJV, emphasis added)? Could God be *that* good?

No Greater Power

"He shall save" is not only a prophetic statement made at the beginning of Jesus' life on earth, but it was also an in-your-face power statement made by the God of the universe. It was an emphatic statement of fact. Bishop Rick Hawkins, speaking under a pew-shaking anointing of the certainty of God's will and ability to save, said the following:

> What will he save us from? He will save us from sin. Now automatically two perspectives come into this building. The word *sin* brings a horrid, horrible feeling. It's like we revere sin more than we revere the Savior. It's almost like we're so scared of sin that we put sin up as a rival to the Savior.
>
> I'm going to shake some of your theological cages today. I'm going to minimize sin for you. Sin has never been as powerful as grace. For my Bible tells me where sin abounds, grace did much more abound. I'm sorry to shatter your image of sin. I'm sorry to destroy your reverence of sin, like sin is set up over here with the same amount of power as grace. Sin has never been even comparable to grace. It can't even get on the same ball field; it cannot even inhabit the same office. When grace walks in, sin walks out.
>
> You need to get a new perspective. Sin is not all that. Grace is all that. Jesus said, "I came specifically to save." He will save. Somehow we think that sin has a chance against the Savior. I came to tell you that sin doesn't have a chance against the Savior. Sin doesn't have a chance against Jesus. Sin only has a chance against your mind. (Bishop Rick Hawkins, Place for Life, December 23, 2007)

I have made a choice. I choose to make the case for "He will save" as opposed to sin defeating humankind. I refuse to maximize the power of sin and minimize the power of God's grace. I choose to interpret scripture from the perspective of the eternal plan for victory. Sin, death, hell and the grave were defeated at Calvary and remain defeated to this very day— the defense rests – the case is closed. I wager that the power of God is greater by far than the power of Satan. Say these words until the revelation of God's great power breaks through: "He will save! He will save! He will save! He will save!"

What God Counts

Okay, let me confess. At this point, it would be easy to think that it's too good to be true to believe that the wicked and unbelieving were saved, are being saved, and will be saved. And you know what they say, "If it's too good to be true…" But then I remember the scripture that says, "Abraham believed God and God counted it to him for righteousness" (Genesis 15:6 KJV). A few millennia later, this verse is repeated in the New Testament: "What does the Scripture say? 'Abraham believed God, and it was credited [*counted* in the KJV] to him as righteousness' " (Romans 4:3). That seems a little more believable because it says Abraham *believed* God. But the operative word in the passage is *counted*. This suggests that Abraham's believing, though important, was not the trigger. Rather, it was in the way God counted.

Look further with me. Romans 4:5 says, "And to the one who does not work but believes in him who justifies the ungodly, his faith is counted as righteousness" (ESV). Combine this with what used to be my least favorite scripture in the Bible, Isaiah 64:6: "But we are all as an unclean thing, and all our righteousness are as filthy rags; and we all do fade as a leaf; and our iniquities, like the wind, have taken us away" (KJV). It is clear to me that the implications of these scriptures are testimony to a love like no other.

I conclude that we don't stop sinning to get saved, but we get saved so we can stop sinning. We are not saved because we are righteous, but we are saved because His death paid our debt and He counts us righteous. "For he hath made him to be sin for us, who knew no sin; that we might be made the righteousness of God in him" (2 Corinthians. 5:21 KJV).

God's accounting system is not a meritorious one in which we must pass a test to gain favor and position. I don't know altogether what or how He counts. But today I believe He counts in a way that transcends most of the earthly barriers, circumstances, calculations and conditions. How and what God sees and counts is very different from the way we see and count. The Bible says, "We don't yet see things clearly. We're squinting in a fog, peering through a mist. But it won't be long before the weather clears and the sun shines bright! We'll see it all then, see it all as clearly as God sees us, knowing him directly just as he knows us!" (1 Corinthians 13:12 MSG) We have a double problem – we see dimly and God sees differently. God views us through blood colored glasses since the day Jesus died on our behalf. We see our past. We see and judge the moment. God sees us as we were purposed in eternity. He sees and counts potential and destiny. He told Jeremiah: "Before I shaped you in the womb, I knew all about you. Before you saw the light of day, I had holy plans for you: A prophet to the nations—that's what I had in mind for you." (Jeremiah 1:5 MSG) Jeremiah became the prophet God ordained him to be but not without a few inglorious bouts of complaining, whining and weeping, Please note that God did not count his weakness as disqualifying. He looked beyond his faults and saw His purpose. God is not committed to orthodoxy. He is committed to His purpose. As Jesus told the disciples, God's purpose is not to kill us but to save us.

When we casually stand in a prayer line as we wait to be anointed, He counts it as saving faith, comparable to confessing Christ and believing that God has raised Him from the dead. When we cry out in desperation for God's help, God counts it as a confession of faith, even though we may be full of sin. When a Chinese peasant woman giving birth screams *Shangdi* (which literally means "above emperor"), the someone she believes is above the emperor—God—hears her and counts it as righteousness. When a defenseless eight-year-old Tutsi girl in Rwanda is being gang-raped by soldiers, and her screams are no longer audible, and she mumbles words that translate into no known language, God hears her and counts it as her confession of faith. And what is more, if she never cries out, God hears her anyway because His blood was shed for her—my Western Holiness theology notwithstanding.

When we acknowledge God by saying grace before we eat, God smiles and hears it as a confession of faith and thanksgiving. When we arrogantly acknowledge that what we just said or did was wrong and "God is just gonna have to forgive me," the holy God laughs, forgives, and counts our speaking to Him as faith. Call it cheap grace, if it makes you feel more spiritual or biblically correct, but I think it's better than cheap—it's free grace. In the end, it is not how we say it or what we say; it is His sovereign, arbitrary, unconditional love and what *He* purposes that *counts*.

One more thing: What about Abraham's faith and the person like him who does not work for salvation but believes? Are these preconditions? Well, consider this: First of all, grace and faith are gifts from God; they don't come from us (Ephesians 2:8). Second, God counts us righteous while we are yet unrighteous (Romans 5:8). Additionally, Romans 6:11 says we are to count ourselves as dead to sin. If God counts me righteous and tells me to count myself righteous, I am not going to argue my unworthiness or anybody else's. I'm going to accept my unworthiness as a foregone conclusion and embrace the new lifestyle that awaits me as a new man in Christ, where old things have passed away and all things have become new (2 Corinthians 5:17), where I become the righteousness of God - in Him.

Yes, that's right, despite all my baggage, despite all my arrogance and bad habits, despite both my good and bad intentions; my good days and bad days, I am righteous - in Him. "God made him who had no sin to be sin for us, so that in him we might become the righteousness of God" (2 Corinthians 5:21). Not only did Jesus die for my sins and count me as righteous, He also said He would be my righteousness. Wait, somebody pinch me... Could God be *that* good?

What God Does Not Count

While God was counting us righteous in fulfillment of His pronouncement that He would save His people from their sin, He also declared what He would *not* count: "God was reconciling the world to himself in Christ, *not counting men's sins* against them (2 Corinthians 5:19, emphasis added). He does not count our sins.

Here is the ultimate question: are we covered by the blood of God (Jesus) because we placed ourselves under the fountain, or are we covered by the blood of God (Jesus) because He placed the fountain over us? Could this be what is meant in Matthew 5:45, "that ye may be the children of your Father which is in heaven: for he maketh his sun to rise on the evil and on the good, and sendeth rain on the just and on the unjust"?

The ultimate answer is given in one of the most important passages in the Bible:

Saving is all his idea, and all his work. All we do is trust him enough to let him do it. It's God's gift from start to finish! We don't play the major role. If we did, we'd probably go around bragging that we'd done the whole thing! No, we neither make nor save ourselves. God does both the making and saving. He creates each of us by Christ Jesus to join him in the work he does, the good work he has gotten ready for us to do, work we had better be doing.

—EPHESIANS 2:8–10 (MSG)

In Titus 3:5, Paul reinforces this principle I call preemptive grace.

He saved us, not on the basis of deeds which we have done in righteousness, but according to His mercy, by the washing of regeneration and renewing by the Holy Spirit. (NASB)

God is not counting our sins, because of Hebrews 9:26:

Then Christ would have had to suffer many times since the creation of the world. But now he has appeared once for all at the end of the ages to do away with sin by the sacrifice of himself.

Now here is my point: God died on the cross to save, not just Christians, but whosoever would believe (John 3:16). Belief is made possible by an act of God, not by humankind (Ephesians 2:8–10; Titus 3:5), and it is exercised by those He reveals Himself to, whether in a Christian church, Jewish synagogue, Muslim mosque, Buddhist pagoda, or through private revelation. Now that may be a difficult statement for many of us Christians to accept. We have assumed ourselves to be the center of the universe perhaps because we have the advantage of Gods' written Word. However, we have forgotten that that written Word says God so loved the *world* that He gave His only begotten Son.

Again, Romans 1:18–20 explains this for us:

> For the wrath of God is revealed from heaven against all ungodliness and unrighteousness of men, who by their unrighteousness suppress the truth. For what can be known about God is plain to them, because God has shown it to them. For his invisible attributes, namely, his eternal power and divine nature, have been clearly perceived, ever since the creation of the world, in the things that have been made. So they are without excuse. (ESV)

So the wrath of God is revealed, and the grace of God is also revealed. He is both the righteous judge and Jehovah Tsidkenu, The Lord Our Righteousness. He saves what, when, and whomever He wants to save. He saved Adam, the original sinner who plunged all humanity into sin, by shedding the blood of an innocent animal and covering Adam with the animal's skin. From the time of Adam to Jesus, the blood of an animal was the precursor to the perfect sacrifice of the blood of God in the person of His Son, Jesus the Christ, because He will save. Twice after Abraham lied about Sarah; God saved him because - He will save. He saved the unbelieving Ninevites by a prophetic word sent through His vindictive, hateful, disobedient, believing preacher-prophet Jonah because - He will save. He saved the Jews from bondage in Egypt, though He called them stiff-necked and rebellious, because He will save. He saves us all from the calamity of sin and the certain judgment that follows by His immense, incredible, incomprehensible love, leaving His wrath and judgment for the few who actively and utterly refuse His blood-sacrifice covering and who successfully resist and reject His compelling love, grace, and mercy because – He will save.

God's compassion for His creation is compatible with His attributes. The psalmist declares this clearly and forcefully:

> For their heart was not steadfast with Him, nor were they faithful in His covenant. But He, being full of compassion, forgave their iniquity, and did not destroy them. Yes, many a time He turned His anger away, and did not stir up all His wrath; for He remembered that they were but flesh, a breath that passes away and does not come again. How often they provoked Him in the wilderness, and grieved Him in the desert! Yes, again and again they tempted God, and limited the Holy One of Israel.
> — PSALM 78:37–41 (NKJV)

God promises to forget our sins. In Isaiah 43:25, He declares, "I, even I, am he who blots out your transgressions, for my own sake, and remembers your sins no more." In Jeremiah 31:34, He proclaims, "No longer will a man teach his neighbor, or a man his brother, saying, 'Know the LORD,' because they will all know me, from the least of them to the greatest," declares the LORD. "For I will forgive their wickedness and will remember their sins no more." Finally, Psalm 103:12 reminds us, "As far as the east is from the west, so far has he removed our transgressions from us." In all this, He shows—unequivocally—He will save.

CHAPTER 8

AN ACT OF GOD

*All this is done by God, who through Christ changed
us from enemies into his friends and gave us the task of
making others his friends also.*

—2 CORINTHIANS 5:18 (GNT)

Salvation—An Act of God

An *act of God* is defined by *Merriam-Webster's Collegiate
Dictionary* as "an extraordinary interruption by a natural
cause (as a flood or earthquake) of the usual course of events
that experience, prescience, or care cannot reasonably foresee
or prevent." Insurance companies often attempt to protect
themselves from having to pay for certain damages in natural
disasters by invoking the disclaimer of an "act of God." This
means they cannot be held responsible for events in nature beyond
their control.

Ephesians 2:8 may be one of the most important verses in the
Bible for understanding the arbitrary and sovereign will of God
to love and save the world. Ephesians 2:8 suggests He does it by

eliminating human participation and arbitrarily and sovereignly establishing a broad pathway to salvation and reconciliation. When viewed in this way, the salvation of humankind is truly an act of God.

"For by grace are ye saved through faith and that not of yourselves: it is the gift of God;" Ephesians 2:8 loudly proclaims that both the grace that saves and the faith that saves are gifts that are given to all people everywhere and therefore the keys to understanding all scripture as it relates to the salvation of humankind as the ultimate purpose of God. In other words, whatever your hermeneutical method or procedure, if it does not fit the principle of salvation by grace and faith for all, it is spurious and inaccurate.

I would do well to restate a very important premise; that is, that in the New Testament in particular I use principle as a basis for interpretation. Said another way, I do not limit my interpretation of a scripture to the letter of the scripture but primarily to the spirit of the letter. In the Old Testament the letter of the law prevailed. In the New Testament the spirit of the law prevails. It represents a dramatic paradigm shift that influences how we "see," "hear" and understand the Word of God. Paul said, "He has made us competent as ministers of a new covenant--not of the letter but of the Spirit; for the letter kills, but the Spirit gives life." (2 Corinthians 3:6) Therefore, "thou shalt not commit adultery" is expanded under New Testament law to include the principle or spirit of the law "…if a man lusts after a woman, he has committed adultery in his heart". Only God can know if and when adultery is committed in the heart. Man judges the outward appearance but God judges the heart. Likewise, only God knows when one has "believed" sufficiently to be covered by His blood. The Sawi accepted Christ in principle as "The Peace Child" not according to the letter - "That if thou shalt confess with thy mouth the Lord Jesus, and shalt believe in thine heart that God hath raised him from the dead, thou shalt be saved. For with the heart man believeth unto righteousness; and with the mouth confession is made unto salvation." (Romans 10:9-10 KJV) What I am saying is, we cannot apply the letter of the New Testament to every culture and all circumstances in the world, but we can apply the spirit of the New Testament scripture universally.

Therefore, when we look at the framework of salvation we must see the way God sees it and not through the eyes of our limited human understanding with our myriad of theologies and denominations. This is precisely why Paul told the confused Corinthians, "So from now on we regard no one from a worldly point of view though we once regarded Christ in this way, we do so no longer. Therefore, if anyone is in Christ he is a new creation; the old has gone the new has come!" (2 Corinthians 5:16-17 NIV)

Consequently, if grace is unmerited favor anywhere in Scripture, it is unmerited favor everywhere in Scripture. If grace brings undeserved favor to anybody in the world; it brings undeserved favor to everybody in the world. If the thief on the cross without repenting for sins and who only acknowledged Jesus' ability to "remember" him can be saved, then surely the soldiers acknowledgement was equally efficacious when they said, "Surely this man was the son of God" and surely any other seeking soul will be received by that same love and grace the letter of their compliance notwithstanding.

God's standard is stated clearly: "The servant who knows what his master wants and ignores it, or insolently does whatever he pleases, will be thoroughly thrashed. But if he does a poor job through ignorance, he'll get off with a slap on the hand. Great gifts mean great responsibilities; greater gifts, greater responsibilities!" (Luke 12:48 MSG) Interestingly, the Holy God, still "requires all men everywhere to repent" and He still insists that without faith it is impossible to please Him and he that comes to God must believe. These Godly mandates all blend into a sovereign love that recognizes the mitigating human circumstance so when viewed through the eyes of grace and mercy - practice gives way to principle.

Psalmist Clint Brown wrote:

> Where would I be You only know
> I'm glad You see through eyes of love
> A hopeless case, an empty place
> If not for Grace
>
> Amazing grace how sweet the sound
> I once was lost but now I'm found
> A hopeless case, an empty place
> If not for Grace
>
> Precious Lord please take my hand
> Lead me on let me stand
> A hopeless case, an empty place
> If not for Grace

The Father accommodates and facilitates our finding Him. The world does not find him physically; the world finds God by Faith. "Romans 10:13-17 says, "For whosoever shall call upon the name of the Lord shall be saved. How then shall they call on him in whom they have not believed? and how shall they believe in him of whom they have not heard? and how shall they hear without a preacher? And how shall they preach, except they be sent?" God reveals Himself and God causes humankind to believe. First, they believe that He is. Second, they believe that He is a rewarder. And, the reward turns out to be more than they can ask or think. It is everything from rain, to a good crop, to physical healing or returning to our eternal home in heaven. In any case, it is the fundamental purpose and goodness of God to reveal Himself.

Justification – An Act of God

All humankind was cast into sin the moment Adam and Eve partook of the tree of the knowledge of good and evil. Likewise, the justification of humankind happened the instant sin's debt was paid – when Jesus died on the cross. To say that the crucifixion was only an appropriation of justification but not a complete application is an unbiblical human assertion that limits and denies the power of the cross, denies the finished work of the Savior who said, "It is finished," and denies the clear unambiguous oft-repeated Word of God that says as Adam was – Jesus is. To believe that God only "set up" justification but did not justify humankind at the cross is to reject the primary premise of our salvation by grace through faith with none of it of ourselves. Furthermore, God's act to save humankind was not only appropriated but also premeditated, applied and more importantly - passive. Could God be as good as Romans 5:1-2, 8, 9-21 implies?

The greatest most enlightening story of reconciliation is the parable of the Prodigal's Son in the gospel of Luke 15:11-32. The greatest explanation of the doctrine of reconciliation is Romans chapter 5. And the greatest application of the doctrine of reconciliation is 2 Corinthians chapter 5:18-21. In not one of these power scriptures is there an act of humankind reconciling with God. In every passage it is an act of God. God sets the terms, provides the tools and the time. Salvation happens because God supplies the redeeming sacrifice, the faith and the grace.

Consequently, the deaf-mute can be saved; the ignorant wayfarer though a fool can be saved; and "whosoever believes on him..." can and will be saved. Clearly, clearly we are justified by faith in the finished work of our Lord Jesus Christ. That faith is "not of ourselves it is the gift of God, not of works lest any man should boast."

I'm sorry, I know many of us were taught that we had a primary role to play; that we had to have "a made up mind;" that we had to have some skin in the game – some responsibility and perhaps you do in that when faith came as a free gift you accepted it. If God says it is not His will that any should perish but that all should come to repentance then we must expect to see the ways and means in the scriptures that makes coming to repentance a universal possibility. There must be a way that the "wayfarer" and those who do not have access to the Word will without the Word satisfy God's requirement as in 1 Peter 3:1-2 "Wives, in the same way be submissive to your husbands so that, if any of them do not believe the word, they may be won over without words by the behavior of their wives,". The Word of God is crystal clear - inheriting sin was passive. I was born under a curse of sin inherited from father Adam. I had nothing to do with inheriting that original curse. The scriptures are equally clear that Jesus' death removed the curse of sin and I had nothing to do with the removal.

"Therefore as by the offence of one judgment came upon all men to condemnation; even so by the righteousness of one the free gift came upon all men unto justification of life. (Romans 5:18 KJV)

Both sides of the equation are balanced. By that I mean from a state of righteousness man chose sin and likewise from a state of sin man in Christ chooses righteousness. I inherited Adams sin and I inherited Jesus' righteousness. Ephesians takes it a gloriously sovereign-act-of-God step further:

According as he hath chosen us in him before the foundation of the world, that we should be holy and without blame before him in love: Having predestinated us unto the adoption of children by Jesus Christ to himself, according to the good pleasure of his will," (Ephesians1:4-5 KJV)

"God made him who had no sin to be sin for us, so that in him we might become the righteousness of God. (2Corinthians 5:21)

I believe the Word teaches that man must believe and receive. "…In whom after that ye believed ye were sealed…" (Ephesians 1:13c KJV). I do not see this as a significant or insignificant work of man because it is God influencing man to believe with the free gift of grace through faith. So that no matter how you parse it, we are saved by grace people…grace…through faith and neither comes from you the grace and the faith comes from the Sovereign God who says He set the whole thing up "…according to the plan of him who works out everything in conformity with the purpose of his will…" (Ephesians 1:11b).

I say again, how humankind comes to faith in God is not a judgment you will make. Only God must be satisfied according to his plan and purpose for all. So get out of the door. Stop "carding" people (checking ID's). Jesus is the door that no man can open and no man can shut. Put the word out – ALL are welcomed to the table. The meal has been completely prepared. Tell everybody you see, "come on home, God is not holding their sins against them." The penalty for your sins has already been paid. You have already been redeemed. All one has to do is accept the free gift and let the goodness of God take over from there. I am absolutely sure there will be quite a few surprises in heaven. Jeffrey Dahmer - pedophile, necrophiliac, and mass murderer, accepted Jesus Christ before a fellow prisoner beat him to death. An act of God will receive him as it will receive you and me.

Now come on! If you have committed a capital crime and you with many others are sitting on death row waiting to be executed and suddenly some one rushes in with papers in his hand with "JUSTIFIED" stamped across them and announces to all the inmates your penalty has been paid, you are free to go. There is only one thing for you to do...go. You would not wait to make sure, collect property, and finish a meal or a chore. You'd snatch the paper out of his hand and go. You are free and you did nothing to get yourself free. It is indeed incredible and it may even be too good to be true; you might feel unworthy but as you deal with those feelings you are headed for the door and the daylight. You wonder who sprung you, why and how - who would do such a thing? But the bottom line is you are justified. You are free. There is no record of a crime ever being committed. It's just as if you never did it. Whoever died to pay for your sin didn't do it "with" you He did it "for" you. We don't know when or how you reacted. You may have wept both for joy and sorrow. Joy that you are free (justified) and sorrow swearing you'll never do what you did again (repentance). What we do know is that faith is followed by acceptance; acceptance is followed by repentance which is the natural response to the goodness of God.

We must not be conflicted or confused by the salvation formula. The recitations of various oaths, confessions of faith, The Apostle's Creeds, the Four Spiritual Laws, The Sinners Prayer, right hands of fellowship, baptisms, etc, etc., are not magic formulas that save us or seals the deal. They may be important commemorations, celebrations and public confessions that announce our coming into faith but they do not justify us. Again, justification in particular and salvation in general comes by grace through faith and neither the grace nor the faith comes from us. (Ephesians 2:8)

Not only does God save His creation by grace through faith, He also is the engineer of lifestyle change through confession and repentance. Grace, faith, confession and repentance are the four pillars of salvation.

The term repentance in the original Greek is the word *metanoia*, which means "to turn from and turn to"; it implies a transformative change of heart and change of mind. To repent, then, is to have a change of mind that leads to a change of behavior, which, according to 2 Corinthians 7:10, "leads and contributes to salvation and deliverance from evil, and it never brings regret." Repentance is commanded by God but it is a benefit for us. What am I driving at? As humans we are not in charge of the - how. These components are parts of the whole – the whole being full salvation. The sequencing cannot always be observed. The doctrinal catechisms and theological protocols of our religious institutions are not always followed by the Spirit-driven purpose of God. What we know for sure is that we were called to full salvation and the lifestyle of holiness and this call came before the foundation of the world. The Apostle Paul writing to the church in Ephesus said:

> How blessed is God! And what a blessing he is! He's the Father of our Master, Jesus Christ, and takes us to the high places of blessing in him. Long before he laid down earth's foundations, he had us in mind, had settled on us as the focus of his love, to be made whole and holy by his love. Long, long ago he decided to adopt us into his family through Jesus Christ. (What pleasure he took in planning this!) He wanted us to enter into the celebration of his lavish gift-giving by the hand of his beloved Son.

> Because of the sacrifice of the Messiah, his blood
> poured out on the altar of the Cross, we're a free
> people—free of penalties and punishments chalked
> up by all our misdeeds. And not just barely free,
> either. Abundantly free! He thought of everything,
> provided for everything we could possibly need, letting
> us in on the plans he took such delight in making. He
> set it all out before us in Christ, a long-range plan
> in which everything would be brought together and
> summed up in him, everything in deepest heaven,
> everything on planet earth. (Ephesians 1:3-10 MSG)

Our salvation was not a counteraction to anything done by
Satan or us. It was fully preconceived in eternity and carried out
in time. Satan lured us away from the Father with a powerfully
suggestive lie. Now turn to your neighbor and say, "BUT GOD!"
God won us back with a love more powerful than Satan's lie. He
loved us with a love that caused Him through Jesus to die on the
cross and redeem us from death, hell and the grave. He revealed
Himself through Jesus, The Word. "Faith comes by hearing and
hearing comes by the Word of God." (Romans 10:17 KJV) Hear
it again:

> It wasn't so long ago that you were mired in that old
> stagnant life of sin. You let the world, which doesn't
> know the first thing about living, tell you how to live.
> You filled your lungs with polluted unbelief, and then
> exhaled disobedience. We all did it, all of us doing
> what we felt like doing, when we felt like doing it,
> all of us in the same boat. It's a wonder God didn't
> lose his temper and do away with the whole lot of us.
> Instead, immense in mercy and with an incredible
> love, he embraced us. He took our sin-dead lives and
> made us alive in Christ. He did all this on his own,

with no help from us! Then he picked us up and set
us down in highest heaven in company with Jesus, our
Messiah. (Ephesians 2:1-6 MSG)

Clearly, it is the Father's divine strategy to initiate reconciliation
by loving us back to Him. Men and women all over the world
are provoked by that love to believe in Him, even when they
don't know His name or call Him by different names. There's a
reason there are more believers than atheists. Even though many
have not been exposed to organized religion, God has revealed
Himself enough for most to believe there is a God. God's love
for the world has created the pathway out of darkness without
the religious orthodoxy most of us are accustomed to. Then, in
direct proportion to the revelation of God's love and goodness,
comes ongoing repentance, conversion and worship. I know that
God's Word is the standard for the world; however, I don't know
all His standards of application. I also know to whom much is
given, much is required; and likewise, to whom little is given,
little is required.

Just as an insurance company uses the disclaimer of "acts
of God" to protect itself from client claims, so also is it our
claim when the accuser questions our claim of righteousness he
hears our response – it was an act of God. My testimony is I am
saved by an act of God. Therefore, no claim of Satan is valid
because salvation is an act of God. Whether that claim is made
in Saudi Arabia, Asia, Germany, Mississippi, or Bangladesh, it has
been satisfied by Jesus' victorious proclamation of justification.
Whatever issue Satan or theologians may have, they must take it
up with God because the deal is already done. Justification has
been appropriated AND applied. It has been signed in the blood
of God Himself and sealed with the declaration from no greater
love, "It is finished!"

What specifically was the act of God? Jesus died on the cross on humankind's behalf and settled all claims. It's all in the last will and testament, specifically Romans 5:18:

> We see, then, that as one act of sin exposed the whole race of men to God's judgment and condemnation, so one act of perfect righteousness presents all men freely acquitted in the sight of God. One man's disobedience placed all men under the threat of condemnation, but one man's obedience has the power to present all men righteous before God. (JBP)

As awesome as the news of salvation being free and unconditional is, as hard as that is for some to believe, there is late-breaking news even more astounding:

> For if, when we were enemies, we were reconciled to God by the death of his Son, much more, being reconciled, we shall be saved by his life.
> —ROMANS 5:10 (KJV)

Using verses 9 through 11 of Romans 5 as context, the J. B. Phillips translation is breathtaking in scope and implication:

> Moreover, if he did that for us while we were sinners, now that we are men justified by the shedding of his blood, what reason have we to fear the wrath of God? If, while we were his enemies, Christ reconciled us to God by dying for us, surely now that we are reconciled we may be perfectly certain of our salvation through his living in us. Nor, I am sure, is this a matter of bare salvation—we may hold our heads high in the light of God's love because of the reconciliation which Christ has made.

"What reason have we to fear the wrath of God?" Sadly, by reason of the various toxic doctrines of our religious traditions that constantly tell us that what Jesus did at Calvary was not enough. But, I promise you this day, the news is better than most of our religions have taught us: you need not fear; the work has been done for us. The only thing left for you to do is to embrace your salvation. Therein lies the mission of every Believer – to connect the world to its destiny "in Christ."

The best news you have ever heard in your life is that you were placed in Christ before the foundation of the world. When Christ went to the cross, you went with him. When he died, you died. When he arose, you arose. He has become sin for us that we might become the righteousness of God. Take the deal! Quit play'n and say "YES"…RIGHT NOW!

Hold on to your seat again—you won't hear this in Sunday school! Is God, through His apostle, saying that we are saved before we ever open our mouths? Is God saying we are saved first and converted second? Did we get justified at the first altar – the cross - and converted at the second altar at church, in your kitchen, at youth camp, in a foxhole or wherever the "connection" came or you prayed "the sinner's prayer?" Did my salvation process begin at the cross and end at the altar. Does the order really matter… really?

Romans 5:8 clearly says, "God commendeth his love towards us, in that, while we were yet sinners, Christ died for us" (KJV). Verse 10 in the J. B. Phillips translation says, "we can then be perfectly certain of our salvation because we have been reconciled by His death." There it is again—salvation is an act of God. God kept His word, and Satan's head has been crushed by the seed of the woman (Mary, who birthed Jesus Christ). God wins! All the religions of the world notwithstanding, the death and resurrection of God in Jesus has trumped them all and prevailed. We were saved. We are saved. We will be saved! I was the one drowning, unable to save myself. Is God really that good?

James Rowe said it well in his now famous hymn written in 1912, "Love Lifted Me":

> I was sinking deep in sin, far from the peaceful shore,
> Very deeply stained within, sinking to rise no more,
> But the Master of the sea heard my despairing cry,
> From the waters lifted me, now safe am I.
>
> Refrain:
> Love lifted me!
> Love lifted me!
> When nothing else could help,
> Love lifted me!

It is crystal clear. You were reconciled to God before the altar, not at the altar or after the altar (for those of you who "got saved" in an old-fashioned go-to-the-altar-after-the preached-Word church). You were justified before your first communion or before you were baptized in water and came up speaking in tongues... or not. The church (or wherever) altar was then the place of your believing, confessing and repenting. The earthly altar was where you were "born again." It was your moment in time – your place of accepting the deal. The fix was in before you were baptized by sprinkling or submersion or before you "joined church" and started paying your dues, tithes, penance, or whatever. Regardless of the religious ritual you went through to demonstrate to yourself and others that you were "in," the work of justification, in particular, and salvation in general, was already accomplished when Jesus announced on the cross, "It is finished!" In the words of the gospel song by Shirley Caesar, "Somebody hold my mule!"

Listen to that Good News from the reader-friendly Message translation yet again:

> Now that we are set right with God by means of this sacrificial death, the consummate blood sacrifice, there is no longer a question of being at odds with God in any way. If, when we were at our worst, we were put on friendly terms with God by the sacrificial death of his Son, now that we're at our best, just think of how our lives will expand and deepen by means of his resurrection life! Now that we have actually received this amazing friendship with God, we are no longer content to simply say it in plodding prose. We sing and shout our praises to God through Jesus, the Messiah!
>
> —ROMANS 5:9–11 (MSG)

The Works

Now here is where we traditionalists usually get hung up. The role of humans in the plan of salvation and the degree to which salvation depends on us has been an age-old argument for centuries and may still be even in spite of the above few glorious paragraphs. Many of us believe salvation has at least two parts: justification and sanctification. Together, we call them "full salvation." Some call these two components the "two works of grace." Simply stated, it means justification gets us ready to die, while sanctification makes us ready to live.

Full salvation includes both a "works" and a "not of works" side. On the "not of works" side, salvation indeed comes from the unconditional grace and faith expressed in Ephesians 2:8, and it is "not of works, lest any man should boast" (v. 9 KJV). As Titus 3:5 so clearly declares, "Not by works of righteousness which we have done, but according to his mercy he saved us by the washing of regeneration, and renewing of the Holy Ghost" (KJV).

But there is also the "works" side of full salvation. I call it the "conversion" side. This side includes our behavior and requires our participation. Ephesians 2:10 says, "For we are his workmanship, created in Christ Jesus unto good works, which God hath before ordained that we should walk in them" (KJV). Furthermore, Titus 3:8 says, "This is a faithful saying, and these things I will that thou affirm constantly, that they which have believed in God might be careful to maintain good works. These things are good and profitable unto men" (KJV). Among "these things" are confession, repentance, and the indwelling presence of the Holy Spirit - key elements of full salvation.

Hear it again: First, there is justification, the gift of God. This is the grace and faith that saves us from the penalty of sin. It is the gift that keeps on giving for the rest of our lives. We are made right before God by an act of God. We possess new legal standing because Jesus has satisfied the requirement for justice. As a result, we are exonerated, cleared, released, redeemed, and freed. It is "just-as-if-I'd" never sinned—done, complete, and finished.

It amazes me that some of us prefer a more restrictive way to a more exclusive and less accessible salvation. That stems from our carnal instinct to earn it, to have a personal claim, to share in the miracle and to be in the center, to be equally responsible for our own salvation. But God said, "Not of works, lest any man should boast," so get over yourself! Salvation by grace through faith and not of works sets the precedence that becomes the basis for interpreting all of Scripture relating to humankind's salvation.

Second, there is sanctification, the cleansing by the Holy Spirit that brings about separation from sin and the world as we practice the Word. "Sanctify them through the truth: thy word is truth," says John 17:17 (KJV). Sanctification is initiated by our ongoing confession and repentance, and the baptism and indwelling of the Holy Spirit that enables us to overcome the effects of sin (I won't quibble over the order of these things). These are the "good works" that identify a person as being God's child here on the earth.

Jesus was already God's Son when He asked John to baptize Him (Matthew. 3:13). John, knowing that Jesus was the Holy One, perfect and without sin, at first refused to do it, protesting that he was unworthy and in need of being baptized by Jesus. Jesus responded, "Suffer it to be so now: for thus it becometh us to fulfill all righteousness" (Matthew. 3:15 KJV). Did you get that? Jesus fulfilled all righteousness. All the right things, all the qualifiers, were fulfilled in Jesus, who then went to the cross (with me in his loins) and sealed it. Similarly, the indwelling of the Holy Spirit enables you and me to fulfill all righteousness, as he did our Savior.

The point is, we are saved by faith alone, but the faith that saves is not alone. You and I come to the Father justified because of the death of Jesus, but we are still unconverted, or unchanged. To activate the living side of the equation, the resurrection side, we must begin by confessing with our mouths the Lord Jesus and believing in our hearts that God raised Him from the dead. Justification is an act of God alone; sanctification is an act of God with and in us.

The original word for saved is the Greek *sozo*, or *soteria*, which means "healed," "delivered," "made whole," or "salvation." How and when anyone expresses belief is known only to the Father, who has said we should not judge anyone from a worldly point of view. Thus, if anyone is in Christ, that is where and when the process of newness begins. What is more, the Spirit of God leads the justified believer, not into a mere moment of change, but into ongoing lifelong conversion: "old things are (present progressive) passed away; behold, all things are (present progressive) become new" (2 Corinthians. 5:17 NKJV). And, if our personal works of righteousness fail? We do not panic, because 2 Corinthians 5:21 rubs victory in the devil's face: "God made him who had no sin to be sin for us." Salvation is an act of God, and we become His workmanship. Salvation includes justification, sanctification, transformation and restoration. Salvation is a comprehensive work/act of God that is both visible and invisible – leaving Jehovah-God as the ONLY true and righteous Judge. Now that's a mighty good God! I trust Him only.

CHAPTER 9

THE GLOBAL ACQUITTAL

Jesus prayed, "Father, forgive them; they don't know what they're doing."

—LUKE 23:34 (MSG)

The Global Deity

S ince the original sin of Adam and Eve, all humanity has suffered under a sentence of death: "But you must not eat from the tree of the knowledge of good and evil, for when you eat of it you will surely die" (Gen. 2:17). I contend that the holy and sovereign God never intended to lose His creation to the one He created as the tester—Satan, the serpent. God's remedy was born in eternity but played out in time. I continue to contend that just as the original sin of Adam convicted the whole world, cursing it and casting it into chaos, so also did the remedy accomplish a global acquittal. Therefore, God's strategy, in all its dispensations and local manifestations, must be viewed as ultimately universal, or global.

For instance, Israel is best seen as a means to an end, not the end itself. The Jews were not chosen because they were Jews; they were Jews because they were chosen. In fact, in Romans 2:28–29, God purposely redefined who is a Jew and in effect changed the paradigm from national to global, thus fulfilling His ultimate goal that all the nations of the earth be blessed. "For he is not a Jew, which is one outwardly; neither is that circumcision, which is outward in the flesh: But he is a Jew, which is one inwardly; and circumcision is that of the heart, in the spirit, and not in the letter; whose praise is not of men, but of God" (KJV).

Abraham became the father of the Jews when he entered into a global covenant with God. The first child of Abraham, Ishmael, entered into the first covenant and received the same "father of a great nation" promise as did his half-brother, Isaac. The fulfillment of this covenant was a process of time and events that caused the reconciliation of humankind to move past the natural as racial Jews and embrace the supernatural as spiritual Jews.

God has always been about the world. He's too big to be just about the Baptists, the Methodists, the Catholics, the Hindus, the Muslims, the Buddhists, or any other particular religious group. He sits in eternity and works His will universally. He speaks perfect Mandarin Chinese, and He's fluent in the Lahnda language of Pakistan, as well as the Telugu and Marathi languages of India. Russian, English, Swahili, Arabic, and the Ebonics of Detroit all come naturally to Him. It is we humans who insist on our own versions of how to interpret our revelations of Him. With great intentions and expectations, we inevitably bring God down to our size with denominational sound bites and twisted interpretations that fit our first knowledge, racial prejudices, traditions, and culture.

The gospel message is about God dying on the cross in payment for the sins of the world—not that the world might become Christian. The purpose of God's death on the cross was not to start the Christian religion, but to reconcile humankind with God. No religion, including Christianity, reconciles us to God. The religion of Christianity is not the gospel. Only the death and resurrection of Jesus (God in the flesh) reconciles us to God. The gospel of Jesus Christ is not that He came to Christians, but that He came to the world. God accepts what He (God/Jesus) did on the cross, not merely what we do at an altar. It is not the "sacrifice" of our not smoking, drinking, committing adultery, fornicating, lying, stealing, killing, divorcing, and such like that God accepts as worthy of salvation. It is only the sacrifice of God's sin-covering blood and the world being "in Christ" that saves.

On January 1, 1863, the Emancipation Proclamation signed by President Abraham Lincoln took effect and eventually freed the slaves. Texas was the last state to comply with the order. On June 19, 1863, six months after the proclamation, General Gordon Granger and two thousand federal troops arrived in Galveston, Texas, to announce and enforce the Emancipation Proclamation in Texas. News of the proclamation had not reached many of the slaves in Texas. Though they were free, many did not know it and were kept bound by masters determined to keep them as slaves. When the good news reached them, along with the two thousand war-ready federal troops to enforce it, the slaves received the news with gladness and finally celebrated their freedom with dancing and shouting in the streets of Galveston and throughout the state of Texas.

When Jesus died on Calvary, He saved the whole world from the slavery of sin and the penalty of death. We who know that are now sent into the world with this Good News of the gospel of Jesus Christ, much as General Granger was sent to Galveston with the good news of the slaves' freedom. As the slaves did not have to sign an agreement to be free – they were *set* free, neither do we have to sign an agreement to be free from the penalty of sin – we were *set* free by God Himself. Our message is "that God was reconciling the world to himself in Christ, not counting men's sins against them. And he has committed to us the message of reconciliation" (2 Corinthians 5:19 NIV).

The good news is that the war is over and all slaves are free, but not everyone knows that. In General Granger's day, some slaves heard the good news immediately and began to live free. Other slaves did not hear the news right away; though they were free, they did not know it. Still other slaves remained with their masters out of fear, illegal bondage, or for the sake of convenience. They were legally free, but they lived beneath their privilege until help arrived to make them free indeed. The same groups exist today in response to the gospel message. Some quickly embrace the good news, others do not know it, and still others live far below their potential. But it is important to note that failure to accept the good news affects quality of life in time and if willful, perhaps life in eternity also.

God equips believers, those to whom He has revealed Himself and who have embraced that revelation, with spiritual gifts and supernatural signs and wonders. These believers are embedded in every culture and in every nation around the world. They are the General Grangers of the kingdom of God sent forth to announce an emancipation proclamation of their own:

> Rejoice and be glad!
> For the blood hath been shed;
> Redemption is finished,
> The price has been paid.
> Sound His praises, tell the story,
> Of Him Who was slain;
> Sound His praises, tell with gladness,
> He liveth again.
> (Hymn: "Rejoice and Be Glad," author unknown)

Our singular mission is to proclaim the good news that emancipation is in effect for the entire world and will remain in effect until He comes again. All slaves (sinners) are free, and a new lifestyle advocated in God's holy Word offers deliverance from the destructive habits learned in the old life.

Your religion or your view of religion is not the good news. Your form of worship, your tradition or ritual, your method of baptism, or your belief about communion is not the message you are commanded to carry to the world. There is a global message in 2 Corinthians 5:19, but far too often there is a limited, narrow message in the catechisms of our denominational views of that global message.

Cause and Effect

Since the beginning of time, we have had thousands of years to muddle the message. We are millennia removed from the simplicity of the cause of our alienation and the simplicity of the message of reconciliation. From the beginning, it was God's creation, God's human race, and God's laws that governed the creatures on God's earth. When humankind sinned, it was God's justice that had to be satisfied, and it was God's strategy that satisfied the demands of God's own justice. What was the law that was broken? It was man's fundamental, premeditated disobedience represented by partaking of the fruit of the tree of the knowledge of good and evil. Urged on by Satan, the serpent, man staged a mutiny.

What had God declared would happen if Adam violated His command? In a word, "death". "But you must not eat from the tree of the knowledge of good and evil, for when you eat of it you will surely die" (Gen. 2:17). The soul that sins must die.

It is important to understand that the penalty of death was not given because God was angry. He did not say, "I will kill you." He said, "You will surely die." Death was a consequence, not a punishment. God is the source of life; death is the absence of life. Adam's disobedience was a pulling away, an unplugging from his life source in order to obtain the forbidden fruit. Death, then, was a function of Adam's unplugging from his life source. God's warning that Adam would die was His attempt to protect him from an evil consequence that he did not know, since he was created holy with only the knowledge of *good*. What I'm trying to say is that death was a consequence of behavior, not a punishment for misbehavior.

Death was a consequence of disobedience. Adam was created in the image of God; in his original state, he was perfectly holy. He could learn evil only by partaking of the fruit from the tree aptly named "the knowledge of good and evil." When he did, he died, in the sense that death meant separation from his life source.

God and man shared an absolute holiness that permitted absolute, unbridled, and unlimited fellowship. Man was a "little *g*" god, with access to the supernatural. The animals and the elements were globally subject to him. He wielded dominion in and over the entire earth. The instant man disobeyed, however, he lost the ability to share space and enjoy open access with the supernatural relationship.

Immediately Jehovah triggered a plan designed in eternity to recover, restore, and win back His creation fair and square. However, in order for the buyback to meet the requirements of justice, the innocent must die for the guilty. Since all humankind inherited Adam's sin and was therefore born guilty, the question was, who was qualified to die for the guilty? Only the holy God was qualified.

The remedy to justify fallen humanity was created in eternity before the foundation of the world, and its earthly process was first announced in Genesis 3:15. The process was always inclusive and global. The complete and global acquittal of humankind would be consummated at a place and a time determined by God. The place was called Calvary, the time 3:00 p.m., the date Friday, April 3, AD 33. Jesus, God in the flesh, was crucified; and at the precise moment of His death, Jesus, Emmanuel (which means "God with us"), the Christ, the Word, and God the Son shouted from the cross with a voice of triumph—"It is finished!"

It *is* finished. The deal *is* done. The war between good and evil, God and Satan, *is* won. The slamming of the gavel in heaven by the judge of all humankind caused an earthquake on earth that reverberated in hell. Graves on earth burst open, the veil in the temple was rent from top to bottom, and the separation between God and man was bridged. The fix was in.

The crucifixion was the act of God that acquitted, justified, and reconciled man to God worldwide. It is the foundational work of salvation, and it is comprehensive and multifaceted. It includes the love of God. It includes God's gifts of grace, faith, and forgiveness. It includes the seal of God, "the Holy Spirit of promise, who is the guarantee of our inheritance" (Ephesians 1:14 NKJV). It includes the fundamental but varied worldwide human responses of repentance and worship acceptable to God and God alone.

The question for the curious then becomes, how does the world with all its differences of language, culture, and religion find the common denominator that saves? The answer is "in Christ." Just as we were in Adam's loins when Adam sinned, so also were we all in the loins of Christ, the second Adam, when He died on the cross. When Christ died, the world died with Him. When He rose, the world rose with Him.

Please do not grow weary of this power passage of Scripture. It is key to how God saves the world and therefore bears repeating:

> So from now on we regard no one from a worldly point of view. Though we once regarded Christ in this way, we do so no longer. Therefore, if anyone is in Christ, he is a new creation; the old has gone, the new has come! All this is from God, who reconciled us to himself through Christ and gave us the ministry of reconciliation: that God was reconciling the world to himself in Christ, not counting men's sins against them. And he has committed to us the message of reconciliation. We are therefore Christ's ambassadors, as though God were making his appeal through us. We implore you on Christ's behalf: Be reconciled to God. God made him who had no sin to be sin for us, so that in him we might become the righteousness of God.
>
> —2 CORINTHIANS 5:16–20 (NIV)

In the worldly point of view, people judge the outside, but in the kingdom of God, God judges the heart (1 Samuel 16:7). The worldly point of view says that Jesus came to save Jews and Christians, but the kingdom-of-God view says God sent Jesus to save the whole world (John 3:16). The worldly point of view is that only those who have confessed Christ as personal Savior are "in Christ," but in the kingdom of God, since we were all in Adam and therefore born in sin, so also are we all in Christ, the second Adam (1 Corinthians 15:45–47). Jesus, in fact, died for all. God, in fact, was in Christ also and reconciled us to Himself.

In Christ

Now don't miss the part that says "if anyone is *in* Christ." The prerequisite is that we be in Him, not that He be in us. This is important because of the bounty of benefits we receive by being in Christ and the implication that He brings us into the kingdom of God, not that we bring ourselves.

This two-word expression has even greater implications when we remember that Jesus, the Christ, is not the Savior of Christians only, but the Savior of the entire world. He came to save the world. God was in Christ, reconciling the world. In Luke 9:20, Jesus is called "the Christ of God" (NKJV). He is not called the Christ of Christianity. He is God's Savior and has been so from before the foundation of the world.

So, how do we get "in Christ"? According to Scripture, we are chosen in Him in eternity. Ephesians 1:4 says we were chosen by God to be in Him "before the foundation of the world" (KJV). Second Timothy 1:9 says, "Who hath saved us, and called us with an holy calling, not according to our works, but according to his own purpose and grace, which was given us in Christ Jesus before the world began" (KJV). God's purpose and grace were given to us in Christ before the world began—before we were even born. All that would be given in order to restore us to eternal righteousness would come through Christ, and this was the purpose and plan of God established in eternity.

This is consistent with Psalm 139:16: "You saw me before I was born. Every day of my life was recorded in your book. Every moment was laid out before a single day had passed" (NLT). This must be clear in the heart and mind of every human being: we were placed in Christ in eternity. This claim preempts any and all religions, theologies and doctrines that follow.

I know the notion of God successfully saving the whole world is a stretch for some of us. Our knowledge of Him has been passed through the filters of various religions, including the many denominations and sectarian divisions of Christianity. God's sovereign power to bestow a love and grace that did not originate with humankind is almost incomprehensible. And that is precisely why I trust God's broad and eternal plan to save His creation—it carries the wonder of incomprehensibility – only God could pull this off.

There is no human fingerprint on God's plan to save humanity. It is, after all, supernatural. That the love of God could save the whole world in one act of the innocent dying for the guilty—past, present, and future—is incomprehensible. But that's because the plan of salvation comes from an infinite wisdom. The *how* of God's ways and means is often beyond human intelligence. But, to the infinite God, all finites are equal. The psalmist understood this when he declared, "Such knowledge is too wonderful for me; it is high, I cannot attain unto it" (Psalm 139:6).

All of humankind is in Christ, but some have more revelation than others. As we grow in Him, we begin to discover the bounty of benefits that are both individual and universal. For instance, being in Christ means we are unconditionally, inseparably, everlastingly, and globally loved by God:

> For I am convinced that neither death nor life, neither angels nor demons, neither the present nor the future, nor any powers, neither height nor depth, nor anything else in all creation, will be able to separate us from the love of God that is in Christ Jesus our Lord.
> —ROMANS 8:38–39 (NIV)

Chief among the benefits of being in Christ are redemption, forgiveness, and the fulfilling of God's sovereign purpose. No scripture in His Holy Word describes this better than Ephesians 1:7–10:

> It is through the Son, at the cost of his own blood, that we are redeemed, freely forgiven through that

full and generous grace which has overflowed into our lives and opened our eyes to the truth. For God had allowed us to know the secret of his plan, and it is this: he purposes in his sovereign will that all human history shall be consummated in Christ, that everything that exists in Heaven or earth shall find its perfection and fulfillment in him. (JBP)

Forgiveness

The entire purpose of Jesus' coming to the world was to secure global forgiveness on behalf of all humankind. Consequently, the graces that accompanied His purpose were global. Forgiveness was expressly extended to all who "don't know what they're doing" (Luke 23:34 MSG).

Receiving forgiveness and extending it to others are the most cherished graces on earth. According to the *Encarta World English Dictionary*, to be *forgiven* is to be "excused for a mistake or wrongdoing; to have an obligation cancelled, such as a debt." The word *pardon* is synonymous with *forgive*.

Since the fall of Adam, man has had a predisposition to sin. Romans 3:23 says, "All have sinned and come short of the glory of God." Psalm 58:3 reminds us that from our earliest existence, we come forth speaking lies. Thus the concept of God's forgiveness becomes key to human existence.

The terms *forgive, forgiveness,* and *pardon* describe not only God's love for the crown of His creation, but also His strategy for saving it. His great love drives His forgiveness, and His forgiveness is His greatest gift to man. I cannot overemphasize the importance of the word *forgive* and its powerful and principal implications. Perhaps everything I am saying hinges on an accurate understanding of both its definition and its Scriptural context.

In the Old Testament, two primary Hebrew words are translated as "pardon," "pardoned," "forgive," "forgiveness," "forgiven," or "forgiving." These are *nasa* and *salah*. Harris, Archer, and Waltke say, "'Nasa' means the taking away, forgiveness or pardon of sin, iniquity and transgression. So characteristic is this action of taking away sin, that it is listed as one of God's attributes (Exodus 34:7; Numbers 14:18, Micah 7:18)... Sin can be forgiven and forgotten, because it is taken up and carried away" (Harris, Archer, and Waltke, *Theological Workbook of the Old Testament*, Moody Publishers, p. 601).

The prophet Micah asks a wonderfully revealing question:

> Who is a God like you, pardoning iniquity and passing over the transgression of the remnant of His heritage? He does not retain His anger forever, because He delights in mercy. He will again have compassion on us, and will subdue our iniquities. You will cast all our sins into the depths of the sea.
>
> —MICAH 7:18–19 (NKJV)

I love that last sentence, "You will cast *all* our sins into the depths of the sea," because it delivers me from the fear that some of my sins might be so bad they will be retained. After all, that is how human beings do it. It answers the question of whether there might be a difference between intentional and unintentional sin. One writer suggests this is the gospel before the gospel. Tie this in with 2 Corinthians 5:19, that "God was reconciling the world to himself in Christ, not counting men's sins against them," and you begin to get the picture. It makes me want to shout, "Listen up, people. Come on home. God ain't countin' your sins against you. It's already been taken care of!"

The fact is, God's love comes out of eternity from start to finish and is juxtaposed against man's understanding, which comes out of the realm of time. From a human works perspective, the notion that the cross of Christ cured the sin problem—past, present, and future—is understandably mind-blowing and requires at least a small leap of faith to embrace a grace that seems too good to be true. Nevertheless, our time-based handicap notwithstanding, the rich blood of the God of eternity covers all manner of sin and sinner, from the beginning of time to the end of time. *God is that good.*

Numerous verses in the New Testament use the word *aphiemi*, which means "to forgive," "to send away," "to be forgiven." The latter part of James 5:15, for example, says, "If they have sinned, they will be forgiven." Additionally, 1 John 1:9 says God is "faithful and just and will forgive us our sins," and reveals how we can obtain complete forgiveness for any sin we commit, even after becoming believers. (When you come from the Holiness tradition of "sinless perfection," as I do, the idea that one sins after one believes is hard to get over.)

God's Unorthodox Forgiveness

But perhaps the most powerful statement that presents forgiveness as a unilateral and unconditional act of God is 1 John 2:12: "I write unto you, little children, because your sins are forgiven you for his name's sake" (KJV). The operative phrase is "for his name's sake," and the implication is clear. We are forgiven, not because we asked, not because we believed, not because we repented, but because of His name alone.

Romans 4:7 relates to new creations in Christ and says, "Blessed are those whose lawless deeds are forgiven" (ESV). In the original Greek, the phrase "are forgiven" is in the perfect tense, which means the action is ongoing. In other words, God forgave all our sins, and we continuously live in a state of having been forgiven.

Forgiveness is a global, God-initiated gift. No one in the world earns it or deserves it. According to Micah 7:19, He will cast *all* our sins into the depths of the sea; and according to 2 Corinthians 5:17, if *anyone* is in Christ, he is reconciled to God because God was in Christ! How cool is that? The principle is clear: all the sins of any and every person are paid in full because of Jesus.

As God was in Christ forgiving, I was in Christ being forgiven, because "as by one man's disobedience many were made sinners, so by the obedience of one shall many be made righteous" (Romans 5:19 KJV). Furthermore, according to Psalm 23:6, I will dwell in the Lord's house forever because His goodness and mercy will follow me. Two of the most glorious attributes of God, His goodness and His mercy, are in pursuit of me, following me wherever I go; stalking me throughout time. Could God be *that* good?

Forgiveness has been appropriated by an act of God. Just as I didn't cause the world to fall into sin (Adam took care of that), neither did I cause the human race to be cured from the disease of sin (Jesus took care of that). I am forgiven, not as a result of anything I have done, but as a result of what Jesus has done. I receive forgiveness. It has already been abundantly appropriated. By the time I ask for forgiveness, it's already done.

Perhaps God's forgiveness is best demonstrated in five real life events: the woman at the well in John 4:1-42; the woman caught in the act of adultery in John 8:1-11; the convicted and condemned thief on the cross in Luke 23:42-43; the famous moment of God's blanket and gracious forgiveness given in Luke 23:34. And one of the most moving and unorthodox acts of forgiveness is demonstrated in Luke 7:41-50:

There was a certain creditor who had two debtors. One owed five hundred denarii, and the other fifty. And when they had nothing with which to repay, he freely forgave them both. Tell Me, therefore, which of them will love him more?"

Simon answered and said, "I suppose the *one* whom he forgave more."

And He said to him, "You have rightly judged." Then He turned to the woman and said to Simon, "Do you see this woman? I entered your house; you gave Me no water for My feet, but she has washed My feet with her tears and wiped *them* with the hair of her head. ⁴⁵ You gave Me no kiss, but this woman has not ceased to kiss My feet since the time I came in. You did not anoint My head with oil, but this woman has anointed My feet with fragrant oil. ⁴⁷ Therefore I say to you, her sins, which *are* many, are forgiven, for she loved much. But to whom little is forgiven, *the same* loves little."

Then He said to her, "Your sins are forgiven." And those who sat at the table with Him began to say to themselves, "Who is this who even forgives sins? Then He said to the woman, "Your faith has saved you. Go in peace. (NKJV)

I believe many men and women boys and girls of all nationalities, races and religions around the world are saved in equally unorthodox, unscripted encounters just like the woman in this true story.

God through Jesus defied religious custom and social protocol to set a new precedent regarding His will and capacity to forgive; and most importantly none who received forgiveness asked for it. The next time you think you have experienced the unforgivable, remember when Jesus said, "Father forgive them… " he was being crucified on a cross as an innocent man - yet, he forgave the guilty for their crime against himself and he forgives the guilty for their crimes against each other.

I am pleased to repeat the announcement, just in case you missed it: "God was in Christ reconciling the *world* to himself, *not counting men's sins against them*" (2 Corinthians 5:19, emphasis added). John 1:29 loudly proclaims for all to hear, "Behold, the Lamb of God who takes away the sin of the *world*" (NASB, emphasis added). It is absolutely clear that God forgives *all* sin *everywhere.*

Many have been held captive to unnecessary anguish, guilt, hopelessness, and despair fomented by toxic religious beliefs that classify sin as bad, awful, or even unforgivable. Just as FBI agents were once trained to detect counterfeit money by mastering all the details of real money, I hope to counter the notion that sins are categorized and classified by describing the greatest love known to humanity—the love of God—and by repeating the theme of Romans 5:20: "But where sin abounded, grace did much more abound" (KJV).

Grace trumps sin—rejoice! In the kingdom of God, where great sin is present, a greater grace abounds—that is, unless you are one of those who believe sin is stronger than grace, the blood of God is weaker than the sin it was shed to cover, and what happens in time outlasts what was done in eternity.

The Bible is clear: "Do you not know that the wicked will not inherit the kingdom of God? Do not be deceived: Neither the sexually immoral nor idolaters nor adulterers nor male prostitutes nor homosexual offenders…" (1 Corinthians 6:9). And again, it is equally clear that where those sins and every other sin abounds, grace does much more abound. Those sins will not inherit the kingdom of God because they will have been forgiven. The fact is, Jesus came to solve the sin problem. He had only one shot at it, so what He did had to cover past, present, and future. Either His grace covers all sin, or it covers none at all. When we stand before God at the judgment, He will not see our sins; He will see the covering blood of Jesus, and we will be dressed in "His righteousness alone, faultless to stand before the throne." (Charles Naylor, Be An Overcomer) Again, problem solved!

King David committed one of the coldest, most heinous crimes in the Bible when he ordered Uriah, one of his most loyal and trusted soldiers, to be sent to his death in order to clear the way for David to maintain a sexual relationship with Uriah's wife. While serious consequences did reverberate throughout David's family until the day he died (there is always real-time consequences to sin), he was forgiven and restored and never stopped being king or a man after God's own heart.

Abraham lied while on his way to becoming the father of faith and participating in perhaps the greatest covenant agreement between God and man. Moses was a murderer and a fugitive from justice when God called him to be the deliverer of Israel from Egyptian bondage. Samson was "a Nazarite of God from birth until the day of his death" (Judges. 13:7), but between birth and death, he was also a flaming womanizer. His life ended in a glorious suicide that led to a monumental victory of Israel over its perennial enemy, the Philistines.

In a cursing rage, Jesus' most trusted disciple, Peter, denied Him, the Christ, Emmanuel, "God with us." Yet upon Jesus' resurrection, He specifically sought out Peter restored and re-recruited him as one of the leading apostles (John 21:17). The man who denied Him became the rock of Matthew 16:18. The woman caught in the act of adultery was saved by the forgiving wisdom of Jesus (John 8:1–11). In John 4, the woman at the well, a five-time divorcee openly living with a man to whom she was not married was transformed by an encounter with Jesus, without a word of condemnation from Him. It is clear that God forgives all the sins of all the people in all the world—every time.

The message that we can come home to the Father because our sins have been forgiven and He is not counting them against us *is* the gospel; and that has got to be the best news anyone has ever heard. It is the only message of Christian ambassadors that is mandated by Scripture (see 2 Corinthians 5:20). Maybe the most life-giving words Jesus ever spoke are the words "Father, forgive them, for they don't know what they're doing." The world is acquitted. *God is that good.*

CHAPTER 10

THE HOLINESS OF GOD

Even before the world was made, God had already chosen us to be his through our union with Christ, so that we would be holy and without fault before him. Because of his love God had already decided that through Jesus Christ he would make us his children—this was his pleasure and purpose.

—Ephesians 1:4–5 (GNT)

O kay, I'm convinced that God is good and His goodness is global. In fact, He is so good He has arranged, through Jesus' vicarious death and resurrection, to save the world without respect to religion, race, education, nationality, culture, economic status, or political perspective. However, going forward, what is my responsibility? Am I held accountable for anything? Is there a right way to live? Are we all held to the same rule of behavior?

At this point, I break ranks with those who are so full of God's love, grace, and forgiveness that they feel exempt from walking in the power of that love, grace, and forgiveness. From the beginning God has commanded: "Be ye Holy for I Am Holy." (Leviticus 19:2) The Bible is replete with commandments that require obedience. Obedience is a response of our love for God and is made possible by the indwelling Holy Spirit. Jesus said it clearly: "If you love Me, keep My commandments" (John 14:15 NKJV). The New International Version says, "If you love me, you will obey what I command."

The responsibility to obey brings us full circle with Adam, who sacrificed paradise by using his free will to disobey God and thus set off this whole mess. Here's the bottom line and the reality of the whole deal: God's grace notwithstanding, there are consequences to both obedience and disobedience. It did not go well with Adam and it will not go well with us if we live in disobedience. Thank God, however, we do have a guarantee in God's Holy Spirit, the Paraclete, the one who dwells in us and runs alongside us to enable us to triumph over the practice of disobedience.

I know for certain that I am saved, loved, and forgiven. I know it because the Word of God says it. Likewise, I know I am called to live holy and righteous before Him in love. I am as certain of my call to live holy as I am of my salvation by grace through faith. In both cases, the Word of God says it, and therefore I believe it.

Here's the good news: First, Jesus has saved us all by grace through faith. Second, He was made sin for us that we might be made the righteousness of God in Him. So get over yourself. It is not about you—it is about Him. Stop worrying as if it all depended on your good behavior or right doctrine. The Bible is clear: you cannot successfully live by the law of Moses. It's not about you and your ability to be good. If *you* had the ability, you would not need Jesus or the Holy Spirit. Besides, it would take away from God's glorious gift of grace:

I suspect you would never intend this, but this is what happens. When you attempt to live by your own religious plans and projects, you are cut off from Christ, you fall out of grace.

Meanwhile we expectantly wait for a satisfying relationship with the Spirit. For in Christ, neither our most conscientious religion nor disregard of religion amounts to anything. What matters is something far more interior: faith expressed in love" (Galatians. 5:4–6 MSG).

Just practice walking in the Spirit, no matter how wobbly, incoherent, and inconsistent you are, and you're good. You're good because God is good. It's all been taken care of. Besides, according to the best textbook about God, the Holy Bible, your righteousness is like filthy rags (Isaiah. 64:6). It's all in the new will and testament, as expressed in 2 Corinthians 5:21. Read it again and rejoice:

> For God made Christ, who never sinned, to be the offering for our sin, so that we could be made right with God through Christ. (NLT)

Holy, Holy, Holy

Jesus is not only our righteousness, He is made so that He might also become our example. The lifestyle of holiness is the antidote to the learned sin-encompassing lifestyle of worldliness. As we become the slaves of righteousness we are freed from a sin-living and sin-loving lifestyle. God is Holy and demands no less of His offspring.

The God Who is good, Whose grace is great, and Whose love has saved the world is also Holy, Holy, Holy. In fact, this characteristic of God is the only characteristic repeated in Scripture in a threefold expression.

The God of the Bible is *Hakkadosh*, the Holy One. He has set the bar for human behavior and has commanded in both testaments that we live holy because He is Holy. His title comes from a word that means "the one set apart as utterly perfect and unique, utterly transcending the realm of the finite, the fallen, and the imperfect." *Hakkadosh,* the Holy One, is absolutely perfect, flawless, and without defect.

Only God is worthy of worship, for He alone is absolutely holy. So separate, unique, sacred and "other" is He, His being has no comparison. His Spirit and His presence penetrate the entire universe. *Kadosh,* or "the holy," implies differentiation. The realm of the holy is entirely set apart from the common, the habitual, or the profane. *Kadosh* holy is singular, awe-inspiring, and even described as "terrible," or dreadful.

Nehemiah said, "I beseech thee, O LORD God of heaven, the great and terrible God, that keepeth covenant and mercy for them that love him and observe his commandments" (Nehemiah 1:5 KJV). Psalm 68:35 reiterates, "O God, thou art terrible out of thy holy places: the God of Israel is he that giveth strength and power unto his people. Blessed be God" (KJV). The prophet Habakkuk, when he heard the sound of God's approach, said, "Thou didst walk through the sea with thine horses, through the heap of great waters. When I heard, my belly trembled; my lips quivered at the voice: rottenness entered into my bones, and I trembled in myself, that I might rest in the day of trouble: when he cometh up unto the people, he will invade them with his troops" (Habakkuk 3:16 KJV). The holiness of God can be absolutely terrifying when isolated from the healing balm of God's mercy and His abundant grace. As God protected Moses from the all-consuming power of His glory, so also does He shield us, by His blood, from His sin-consuming holiness.

The light of God's glory, sometimes called His *Shekinah* glory, is so absolute in its purity that it wields an offensive power that consumes and destroys anything and anyone in His holy presence that is not like Him. Adam was the only human being who ever stood in the direct presence of God. Adam, in his perfect form before his fall, shared this *Shekinah*, or manifest presence of God. Because he was perfectly matched with God in holiness, he could walk with God in the cool of the evenings in the Garden of Eden. When Adam sinned, however, he lost not merely paradise, but also his relationship with God and, more importantly, the *Shekinah* glory he had shared with God. Without this covering, he was naked and unable to come into the presence of God, lest he die instantly. Consequently, he hid himself until God clothed him with an appropriate, though inferior, covering.

An occasion that exemplifies the differentiating holiness of God and the unholy nature of man is seen in Moses' request to see God. With precautionary steps taken to protect Moses from His manifest presence, Jehovah granted the request. Though sheltered in the cleft of the rock and shielded by the hand of God, Moses came away from the encounter with a glow so bright the people were terrified to look at him and begged him to cover his face until the glory of God's presence abated (Exodus 33:18–23).

Once the first tent tabernacle was complete, "then a cloud covered the tent of the congregation, and the glory of the LORD filled the tabernacle, and Moses was not able to enter into the tent of the congregation, because the cloud abode thereon, and the glory of the LORD filled the tabernacle" (Exodus 40:34–35 KJV).

After Solomon completed the second tabernacle, known as Solomon's Temple, the temple was consecrated, not just by the God who is holy, but by the Holy, the *Kadosh*. This was the God who is holy, holy, holy and whose *Shekinah* glory was so powerful that "when Solomon had made an end of praying, the fire came down from heaven, and consumed the burnt offering and the sacrifices; and the glory of the LORD filled the house. And the priests could not enter into the house of the LORD, because the glory of the Lord had filled the LORD's house" (2 Chronicles 7:1–2 KJV).

The pattern is crystal clear. Because of who God is, when He came to earth to save humankind, all that He is came with Him. He was the seed that supernaturally penetrated Mary's womb, fertilized her egg, and embedded itself in the human embryo. Mary then gave birth to the God-man Jesus, in whom all the fullness of the Godhead dwelt in bodily form (Colossians 2:9) and who was incubating the same spiritual power that spoke the world into existence. It was the same power that consecrated and sanctified the first tent tabernacle and Solomon's temple by filling them with His *Shekinah* glory.

Then, at the cross, that same glory was released on the earth as the soldiers pierced the side of the God-man Jesus. The blood and water that gushed forth fulfilled the requirements for humankind's justification, sanctification, and reconciliation with God. It positioned the church, the new family of God, for one final day of consecration, which happened on the day of Pentecost. The church of God, the human temples filled with His glory, became God's kingdom come on earth as it is in heaven. The promise of the Father, the Holy Ghost, was given on that day (Acts 2:1–4).

Here is the bottom line: *Hakkadosh*, the Holy One, and all that His name includes and implies, has chosen us to be His and to be like Him. Therefore, when He who is Holy, Holy, Holy chooses to save me, calls and causes me to be holy, and does it before the world is created, I think the odds are stacked in my favor that when the deal is done—no matter what you or the theological pundits think—it is so. I am saved. I am holy; declared so by God Himself.

One more thing: Not only am I as a believer in the new spiritual nation called the kingdom of God, but the whole "believing" world is also included (John 3:16). Ephesians 1:4–5 sets the bar for the whole earth, not just the Christian part, and the whole earth rocks and reels as it deals with the tension brought on by the citizens of the kingdom of God in the midst of a hostile, unholy and out-of-order world.

Of course there is confusion. Of course there is religious conflict. Of course chaos and argument abounds among mortals as it relates to who is right and who is wrong and even who are the "believers" but here is what I know for sure: God loves the whole world and came in person to save all of it. Before we received the revelation of the new birth, in His book, we were already born again. Before we could announce our own theologies about who was included and who was excluded, He saved. Before we ever confessed or repented of our sins, He saved. Before we could sort out all of His names, He saved. Before we could work through all the rituals and routines developed over millenniums—many of them silly, irreverent, and irrelevant—He saved. Before we could figure out how to serve Him or what was fact and what was fiction, He saved. And before we could stop sinning, He saved.

Ephesians 1:4–5 could be called the core of the Bible, the summary scripture of Holy Writ, the centerpiece of our purpose for living, the everlasting call to creation to be like the Creator:

> Even before the world was made, God had already
> chosen us to be his through our union with Christ,
> so we would be holy and without fault before him.
> Because of his love God had already decided that
> through Jesus Christ he would make us his children.
> This was his pleasure and purpose. (GNT)

The holiness of God is the DNA, or the imprint, of God on humankind. The Christ of God is the reconciler of all creation, and the love of God is the superglue that holds it together and sustains us in this unbelievable grace until it can be believed. His love upholds the creation and the creature until the do-over is done.

Our behavior is relative to our revelation. We are held responsible for what has been revealed to us. When we live in ignorance of God's commands, we are unable to maximize His glory on the earth. When we willfully disobey, we subject ourselves to the consequences of disobedience, and we are chastised by the Father, who chastens those He loves (Hebrews 12:6–8).

Whatever else you might think and regardless of all that you see and hear around you—the confusion that happens when the natural engages the supernatural and the flesh engages the Spirit; the paradoxes, conflicts, contradictions, and wars that rage; the madness, the meanness, the crazy, the obnoxious, the exhilarating, the depressing, the terror, and the horror that strikes; the dogmatic proclamations of the believers, the atheists, the agnostics, the Arminians, the Calvinists, the crazy right, the liberal left, Al-Qaeda, Hamas, or Islam—whatever you might think about hell and who's going there, mass murders and murderers, the global economy, gays and straights, the price of gasoline, world peace, and on and on, one thing is sure: God calls us to be *holy, holy, holy*, and in Christ—and only in Christ—we are.

We are therefore spoiled for righteousness. We cannot sin with impunity. We are being shaped, chastened, and corrected all the day long. First John 3:9 in the Message translation says it clearly:

> People conceived and brought into life by God don't make a practice of sin. How could they? God's seed is deep within them, making them who they are. It's not in the nature of the God-begotten to practice and parade sin.

I am totally understanding and even sympathetic to those who fall into disobedience and misbehavior. To the drinker or the drunk (for those who make a difference), the porn lover, the adulterer, or the gay person, I say, "I understand. I love you, and you are my brother [or sister] in Christ." After all, the Bible says, "Some of you were once like that" (1 Corinthians 6:11 NLT). But look at what the second part of the same verse says:

> But you were cleansed; you were made holy; you were made right with God by calling on the name of the Lord Jesus Christ and by the Spirit of our God. (NLT)

And, by the way, whatever name is used, whatever the language, customs, culture, or system of belief (religion) embraced, He hears.

God is Holy and does not play our little games that debate theologies that make some winners and some losers; and human theologies that justify man's attempt to live according to the flesh and contrary to His clear Word. When that happens, we live beneath our privilege and cannot maximize His power or glorify His name.

The mistake of the church is that we too often believe to not condemn is to condone, and in the process, we initiate our own condemnation. I have decided to love it out rather than fight it out. I will let the Lord sort it out as He sees fit. But as for me, I will err on the side of love. I would rather have mud on my face for handing out mercy than blood on my hands for handing down judgment.

The grace that saves and the faith that brings us to that grace come with the influence of His holiness. Just as it was Joshua's, so also is it our prophetic and evangelistic destiny that "every place that the sole of your foot shall tread upon, that have I given unto you, as I said unto Moses" (Joshua 1:3 KJV). Every time a man or woman filled with the Spirit of God speaks and ministers in the name of the Lord, the glory and the power of God flavor, influence, and engage that environment, setting off a spiritual chain reaction that sows the gift of faith and grace and awakens the knowledge of God in those estranged from Him.

From the beginning of time, humankind was created in the image of the Creator. In eternity, we were called to be holy: "Even before he made the world, God loved us and chose us in Christ to be holy and without fault in his eyes" (Ephesians. 1:4 NLT). However, the most important thing to remember is that humankind is *accounted* holy by the Holy God. Holiness is as much of a gift as is grace.

Another important point to remember is that the holiness of man is accomplished only in Christ. Adam's sin cursed and corrupted both mankind and the earth. Those who came after Adam inherited Adam's sin. Likewise, Jesus' death paid the penalty for Adam's sin and transferred His righteousness to all people in every age. Here are three game-changing verses of Scripture:

> And since we have been made right in God's sight by the blood of Christ, he will certainly save us from God's condemnation. For since our friendship with God was restored by the death of his Son while we were still his enemies, we will certainly be saved through the life of his Son. So now we can rejoice in our wonderful new relationship with God because our Lord Jesus Christ has made us friends of God.
> —Romans 5:9–11(NLT)

Actually, I believe the entire chapter of Romans 5 is the game changer. Note these three points of the passage:

1. We were made right in God's sight by the blood of Christ. We were made right in God's sight the same way we were made wrong in His sight. One man (Adam) caused us to be born in sin. One man (Jesus) caused us to be born again in righteousness.
2. We were reconciled, restored, and will certainly be saved through no act of our own, but through the life of Christ.
3. Jesus' act has made us friends of God again.

The intent of God to save us and make us holy in Him is all made possible through Jesus Christ. No wonder He shouted "It is finished" on the cross. Spiritually speaking, our salvation and sanctification happened instantly. Again, it was checkmate—game, set, match. Jesus hit the walk-off home run on the cross of Calvary. *God is that good*.

Here is that curse-removing scripture again:

> Yes, Adam's one sin brings condemnation for everyone, but Christ's one act of righteousness brings a right relationship with God and new life for everyone. Because one person disobeyed God, many became sinners. But because one other person obeyed God, many will be made righteous.
> —Romans 5:18–19(NLT)

Could it be that in spite of themselves and not because of any action they performed, the sovereign God Elohim has accomplished the salvation of the human beings He created? Did it all happen in the Spirit before it manifested in the flesh as understanding, confession, and repentance? Is this what Titus 3:4–5 means when it says, "When God our Savior revealed his kindness and love, he saved us, not because of the righteous things we had done, but because of his mercy. He washed away our

sins, giving us a new birth and new life through the Holy Spirit"
(NLT)?

Before we ever made it to the altar, He did it. We were covered
by the sin-covering blood of God and declared holy before the
foundation of the world (Ephesians 1:4). So consider carefully and
get this right. He who is *Hakkadosh*—absolutely Holy, perfect,
and without defect—has declared us holy, righteous, and good.
And He has done for us all what He did for Abraham in Romans
4:17: "(As it is written, I have made thee a father of many nations,)
before him whom he believed, even God, who quickeneth the
dead, and calleth those things which be not as though they were"
(KJV).

Should we then conclude through a preponderance of
Scriptural evidence that holiness is a lifestyle that equips us to
reflect His image and gives us the ability to maximized life on
earth as it was in heaven before the foundation of the world? Go
ahead and say it! Shout it with me: *our God is an awesome God!*

Edward Mote described it best when he wrote the timeless
words of his well-known song "The Solid Rock":

> My hope is built on nothing less
> Than Jesus' blood and righteousness;
> I dare not trust the sweetest frame,
> But wholly lean on Jesus' name.
>
> When He shall come with trumpet sound,
> Oh, may I then in Him be found;
> Dressed in His righteousness alone,
> Faultless to stand before the throne.

CHAPTER 11

SO WHO GOES TO HELL?

Then shall he say also unto them on the left hand, Depart
from me, ye cursed, into everlasting fire, prepared for the
devil and his angels.

—MATTHEW 25:41 (KJV)

If God Is So Good...

How often have you heard someone ask, "If God is so good, why is there so much suffering, meanness, and sickness in this world, and how could a good God send people to hell?" In fact, most Christians have wondered about these questions in the privacy of their own minds, though they have not dared to speak them aloud.

The short, unpolished answer is rather simple. God created the world and the first human pair as perfectly good and righteous, and He gave them power and dominion. He also gave them freewill – the power to choose their own way – even to choose against Him. There is no freewill without free choice and their freewill was soon tested by The Tester - Satan. They chose of their own freewill to believe Satan's lie; they mutinied against God and lost paradise. In so doing, they relinquished to the evil one, Satan, the dominion, power, and authority God had delegated to them. Their sin started a chain reaction of negative consequences that has contaminated the whole earth ever since (Genesis 3:14–19) and will continue until God remakes it.

The short, unpolished answer notwithstanding, there is both good news and bad news. The good news is that God saves His creation in spite of itself by coming down to earth in person and paying for the sins of humankind. As Adam had a choice now we have a choice to accept God's remedy free of charge or to crawl out from under their blood covering and accept the consequences. The bad news is that everything ends on the day of judgment, and those who chose not to accept redemption or to be covered by the blood of God and thereby chose to live in open rebellion against God also chose the consequence of hell. Their names will not be found in the Book of Life and they will be thrown into the lake of fire (Revelation 20:15). Of course, my contention is that at least "a vast crowd, too great to count" (Revelation 7:9 NLT) will be found in the Book of Life because of the covering blood of Jesus.

Hell Must Be Chosen

I believe there is a place called hell. I believe it because the Bible, which I believe to be the Word of God, says that such a place exists. However, I hasten to add that I also believe this place called hell is not for those for whom Christ died and frankly, given the Bible's frequent use of hyperbole and metaphors, I'm not all that sure that the descriptions of hell are literal. As clear as the Bible is on the existence of hell, it is equally clear it was not created for you and me. It was created for the devil and his angels (Matthew 25:41.)

Unfortunately, the devil and his angels will be joined by a few human agents who reject Jesus by refusing to help those He calls "the least of these." Note Matthew 25:41–46:

> Then he will say to those on his left, "Away from me, you that are under God's curse! Away to the eternal fire which has been prepared for the Devil and his angels! I was hungry but you would not feed me, thirsty but you would not give me a drink; I was a stranger but you would not welcome me in your homes, naked but you would not clothe me; I was sick and in prison but you would not take care of me. Then they will answer him, "When, Lord, did we ever see you hungry or thirsty or a stranger or naked or sick or in prison, and we would not help you?" The King will reply, "I tell you, whenever you refused to help one of these least important ones, you refused to help me." These, then, will be sent off to eternal punishment, but the righteous will go to eternal life. (GNT)

Okay, I get feeding the hungry and giving drink to the thirsty, but visiting the serial rapist and murderer in prison? Really, Jesus? (Now I feel like Jonah, who didn't want to preach to the enemy Ninevites.) If taken literally, the Matthew passage raises more questions than it answers. But whichever way you take it doesn't diminish the Bible's assertion that there is such a place as hell for the devil, his angels, and a few inhumane others. In the Old Testament, too, such a place is spoken of: "The wicked shall be turned into hell and all the nations that forget God" (Psalm. 9:17).

These passages may be hyperbolic or symbolic, but I'll leave that argument to those who care about such matters. The two passages cited are enough for me. You'll find no argument here. The worst-case scenario is that the wicked who forget God and the inhumane human agents are toast! Got it. Agreed.

But there's one little caveat called Calvary. It is the place where Jesus bled and died and in so doing took my place, pled my case, and set me free from sin, death, and hell. As soon as my Savior shouted from the cross "It is finished!" He said to his Father and our God, "Into your hands I commit my spirit." It was at that moment—triumphant, with all power given unto Him and mighty to save—He broke through the gates of hell, snatched the keys of hell and death (Revelation 1:18), and led a convoy out. He took His seat at the right hand of the Father, began advocating for all humanity, and, according to Ephesians 4:8–9, led captivity captive and passed out spiritual gifts to men and women. With those gifts, His followers began to establish and unify God's kingdom and exercise their restored dominion on the earth as apostles, prophets, pastors, evangelists, and teachers. His kingdom has indeed come, and His will is being done on earth as it is in heaven.

At the moment of Jesus' self-committal into the Father's hands, the sky turned as black as midnight, though it was only midday. A great earthquake thundered, rocks spontaneously shattered, graves burst open, and the righteous dead walked the city streets (Matthew 27:45–54). Verse 54 says, "Now when the centurion, and they that were with him, watching Jesus, saw the earthquake, and those things that were done, they feared greatly, saying, Truly this was the son of God" (KJV).

I'm just sayin', the existence of hell has little to do with those who acknowledge God and His Christ according to their revelation of Him (Romans 1:17–21). It is a non-issue for those included in His beneficent act of granting His grace to humankind.

I cannot explain all the terrifying truths, falsehoods, and interpretations of hell and the many confused teachings about it. I am often puzzled by the glee I hear in the voices of those who teach about hell as if it were the gospel message rather than the fact that Jesus saves us from having to go there. I call them the bad-news bears, the self-appointed prophets of doom and gloom who relish in finger pointing and whose job it is to cause others to live in fear of hell as opposed to living in the joy and love of God.

Who goes to hell? Those who go to hell are those who want to go to hell. Knowing the truth, they willfully defy their own revelation of God, whatever that revelation may be and choose to accept the consequences.

Whitney Houston

I was sitting at a banquet full of preachers and pastors when one of the zealous men of God blurted out his judgment of Whitney Houston, one of the world's greatest singers, who had recently been found dead in her bathtub. He said rather emphatically, "Oh yeah, Whitney is gonna bust hell wide open." He stated that her life was a mess, she was a drug head, and she had no chance of making it to heaven.

My first thought was to argue his theology; after all, we were preachers, and that's what we do. However, I was so tired of arguing about something that is not in my hands or my opponents' hands. I decided instead to get him to look at his own spirit, so I asked him if he had heard her sing "I Love the Lord" in the movie *The Preacher's Wife*, or her comeback song, "I Look to You." I asked if he knew the last song she sang less than twenty-four hours before she died was "Yes, Jesus Loves Me." To each question, he answered no. I then said, "The same God who forgives you also forgives her. She was in Christ, and Christ was her righteousness. Whitney Houston, like some of us, did not need to be forgiven that was already done, she needed to be delivered. She did not embrace her sin, but she did embrace her Savior, and He is mighty to save."

My point is, we have no right to judge anybody. Who died and put us in charge? Scripture is quite emphatic about that: "Who are you to judge the servants of someone else? It is their own Master who will decide whether they succeed or fail. And they will succeed, because the Lord is able to make them succeed" (Romans 4:14 GNT).

I'm going to say it one more time: as God's ambassadors, the only message we are commissioned and authorized to carry is the message of 2 Corinthians 5:19–21:

> That God was reconciling the world to himself in Christ, not counting men's sins against them. And he has committed to us the message of reconciliation. We are therefore Christ's ambassadors, as though God were making his appeal through us. We implore you on Christ's behalf: Be reconciled to God. God made him who had no sin to be sin for us, so that in him we might become the righteousness of God. (NIV)

This is now my single message. I will leave judgment to the Father, Who is the righteous judge and a good God.

So who goes to hell? I don't know—and I don't much care. It is neither my focus nor my message. I am focused only on the message of reconciliation: that God was in Christ, reconciling the world to Himself, not counting our sins. I am certain that nobody will go to hell except those who choose to go there. It will not be by accident or ignorance, for "I have seen something else under the sun: The race is not to the swift or the battle to the strong, nor does food come to the wise or wealth to the brilliant or favor to the learned; but time and chance happen to them all" (Ecclesiastes 9:11). *God is that good.*

Hope of the Righteous

In the end, we will all have bruises and scars received in the fierce battles of life. We will all have stories to tell the angels of battles fought and victories won. We will have come through sickness and disease, troubles and temptations, great trials and tribulations; triumphs and failures; we will have experienced and endured the gamut of unspeakable tragedies and horrific accidents, incidences and losses of all kinds. However, because we chose of our own free will to respond to God's love by accepting the package deal prepared for us before the foundation of the world, we will be saved. The deal was: in exchange for our acknowledgment of God, we received forgiveness and justification. We did not work for it. We did not earn it in any way. It was all a part of an eternal plan played out in time. We made a choice. We believed God. We accepted the deal.

> All of us used to live that way, following the passionate desires and inclinations of our sinful nature. By our very nature we were subject to God's anger, just like everyone else.
>
> But God is so rich in mercy, and he loved us so much, 5 that even though we were dead because of our sins, he gave us life when he raised Christ from the dead. (It is only by God's grace that you have been saved!) Ephesians 2:3-5 (NLT)

George A. Young in 1903 captured our end of life hope in a song called "God Leads Us Along:"

> Sometimes on the mount where the sun shines so bright,
> God leads His dear children along;

Sometimes in the valley, in darkest of night,
God leads His dear children along.

Though sorrows befall us and evils oppose,
God leads His dear children along;
Through grace we can conquer, defeat all our foes,
God leads His dear children along.

Refrain:
Some through the waters, some through the flood,
Some through the fire, but all through the blood;
Some through great sorrow, but God gives a song,
In the night season and all the day long.

I never developed an interest in hell and I don't remember a lot of preaching about hell as a youngster. I suppose it was because of our confidence we were covered by God's grace and therefore studying hell was a waste of time. Consequently, the saints encouraged themselves with songs of hope especially as the end of life approached. I was raised on this song by William G. Schell in 1893:

Life will end in joyful singing
I have fought a faithful fight
Then we'll lay our armor down
Then our spirits, freed from
Earthly ties shall take their happy flight
To possess a starry crown.

CHAPTER 12

UGLY RELIGION

I've told you these things to prepare you for rough times ahead. They are going to throw you out of the meeting places. There will even come a time when anyone who kills you will think he's doing God a favor. They will do these things because they never really understood the Father. I've told you these things so that when the time comes and they start in on you, you'll be well-warned and ready for them.

—JOHN 16:1–4 (MSG)

Re·li·gion—"the service and worship of God or the supernatural: commitment or devotion to religious faith or observance: a personal set or institutionalized system of religious attitudes, beliefs, and practices" (*Merriam-Webster's Collegiate Dictionary*).

Ug·ly—"frightful, dire, offensive to the sight: hideous; offensive or unpleasant to any sense: morally offensive or objectionable" (*Merriam-Webster's Collegiate Dictionary*).

> *Ugly religion*—the frightful, dire, offensive-to-the-sight, hideous, and objectionable service and worship of God, the supernatural, or the institutionalized systems of beliefs and practices that represent Him.

Ugly Relations

Some years ago, shortly after being selected to lead a major branch of my denomination, I was celebrating the installation of a young pastor when one of my spiritual fathers whom I had known all my life, a man I greatly admired and respected, asked to speak with me in an adjacent office. I said, "Sure," and we quietly stepped into the room. With a straight face, he immediately said, "I just want to tell you that *they* (I instantly knew he was included) are not going to help you be successful."

The sheer abruptness of the statement caused my jaw to drop. The implications of the statement were devastating. I had not yet begun to serve in my new capacity and had done nothing to provoke such a statement. I had just given up the tenure and security of a twenty-two-year pastorate. I was preparing to sell my beautiful house located in a beautiful city to move to a cabin in the woods on the grounds of the headquarters.

From that moment on, I grew up. It was only the beginning of what was to come. I was to see up close the ugliness of my religion.

Five years later, my term ended. Though it had been very successful, I chose not to re-up for more of that wonderful Christian meanness, holy dishonesty, and sanctified character assassination that I had witnessed up close. My idealism was destroyed, and my confidence and trust in "the brethren" was shaken to my moorings. I longed for just one of those leaders to approach me and say they were mistaken, they were sorry, or to just talk to me face-to-face as a brother. No one came.

My point is not to vent about my "frienemies" or to appear as a religious martyr searching for vindication. No, it is much the opposite. It was this experience that led me to the certainty of God's unconditional love for everybody. These were good men. To this day, I believe in them. In spite of the fact that they were wrong about me personally, they were not wrong about their personal relationship with God. I am absolutely sure they love God with all their hearts. As John 16:1–4 explains, by attempting to "kill me," they thought they were "doing God a favor... and never really understood the Father" (MSG). In the process, God showed me my own flaws and mistakes that perhaps provoked them and made me the target of their anger. To this day, I see those times as reflecting the besetting sins and weaknesses of the human nature, the very imperfections covered by the blood of Jesus. And, most importantly, the same blood that covers me covers my brothers.

Most of us who have been raised in church or worked for a church have been wounded by friendly fire. Because I was raised in and around church for most of my life, I often say that my sins, my fights, my celebrations, my hardest laughs, and my greatest tears have all happened in church. My faith is not a sanctuary from reality; it is only the mediator. My Christian brothers and sisters are not little angels who say and do the right thing all the time. Some of them had to be delivered from adultery, pornography, fraud or forgiven for divorcing their wives or lying to the government. My theology does not always prepare me for the pain in the pew or the pulpit.

David, too, lamented this painful discovery: "If an enemy were insulting me, I could hide from him. But it is you, a man like myself, my companion, my close friend, with whom I once enjoyed sweet fellowship as we walked with the throng at the house of God." PSALM 55:12–14 (NIV)

I say to David, "I feel your pain." My mentor, Bishop Benjamin F. Reid, once told me, "You haven't lived until you've been lied about." Indeed, my greatest pains have come from my closest friends… who love God as I do.

Ugly Religion

One of life's lingering mysteries is why God suffers the coexistence of good and evil. Why is there a battlefield…inside the church? How is it that the rational shares a stage with the irrational? Perhaps the most inglorious irony of all is that atrocities, wars, sicknesses, hatred, and divisions of all kind surround the gospel of the kingdom of God, which is "righteousness, and peace, and joy in the Holy Ghost" (Rom. 14:17 KJV). Go figure.

We who are the messengers of the gospel are often faced with the question that begins with "if God is so good, then why…" Not only are we asked to give account for the wickedness in the world, but also we are hard-pressed to explain our own complicity. In the battle for dominion, we find ourselves often co-opted and compromised by the sin-borne instinct to self-indulge and self-destruct. Over the centuries, we have been both victim and perpetrator, scarring our witness and confusing our world. We struggle to remain credible and relevant as we fight an evolved image of what I call "ugly religion."

Ugly religion is religion that has been institutionalized to serve its own end. Ugly religions are institutes full of history and traditions that exist to perpetuate mystery and myth, empty hope, fruitless faith, and endless debates about a God to be more feared than loved. Ugly religions are systems of beliefs that are like clouds without rain, evolving to become part of the problem instead of the solution.

Instead of competing with the world for souls, ugly religion competes with itself for power, fame, and fortune. Ugly religion is about dominance, prominence, imminence, money, green rooms, staging, size, and sizzle - only. Ugly religion is human belief systems that fashion God in its own human image, mirroring meanness and depravity, fomenting and promoting the hatred it decries.

Ugly religion condemns gays with epithets and curses, robbing them of human rights in the name of God. Ugly religion joins hateful mobs to protest abortion and becomes the judge, jury, and executioner by murdering those who violate ugly religion's so-called family values. Ugly religion stones to death the woman caught in adultery while allowing the man to go free.

Ugly religion, being impotent to change hearts and minds, gets in bed with government to legislate the morality it cannot influence by the love and power of God, then bows its head in shame when its own immoral behaviors, and racial hatred are uncovered to the ridicule of an unforgiving and unbelieving world. Ugly religion feigns selective sentiment when it appears horrified at the killing of innocent babies but tolerates, perpetrates, and excuses racial hatred.

The truth is, there has never been a time when those who are called by His name were free from the very sins and corruption they railed against. According to our own record, the Holy Bible, from the time of the first man Adam, we who believe have disobeyed, murdered, lied, stolen, waged war, and committed many atrocities—and often in the name of God.

A Hot Mess

Throughout history, religion has been used as an excuse for some of the worst atrocities imaginable. From ancient history to modern history, religion has been, for many people, just an excuse to kill other people. There are even those who claim to be atheist, agnostic, or pantheist ("it will all pan out in the end"; don't laugh—these guys may be on to something) because of the confusion and inconsistency in religion.

What exacerbates the problem, according to David B. Barrett, the researcher who compiles religious population estimates for the World Christian Encyclopedia is the fact that there are about ten thousand distinct religions in the world today. Dr. Barrett identifies ten thousand distinct religions, of which 150 have a million or more followers. Within Christianity (one of twenty major religions), he counts 33,830 denominations. (David B. Barrett; World Christian Encyclopedia; Religion & Science Interface 2002-2005; Page 37)

The sad truth is that many of these religions, and all of the twenty major religions, have been so certain of their authenticity that they have been willing to draw lines of distinction we commonly call "denominations." They then separate themselves from others and kill one another in an effort to keep heretics out or force nonbelievers in. In the community I grew up in, this was called a "hot mess."

Really, is there an acceptable, honorable, holy explanation for the human atrocities committed in the name of God? And do you really think we should live our lives in fear of the words and thoughts of the philosophers, theologians and religious leaders of such evil?

From the Roman persecution of Christians in the first century, to the infamous Christian inquisitions in the tenth and twelfth centuries, to the Islamic jihads, to the insane killing of women who don't wear a burka or who are caught talking to men who are not their husbands, to the Taliban's attempted assassination of a fourteen-year-old girl for advocating the education of females, to the Christian murdering of doctors who perform abortions— religious zealots of one kind or another have terrorized, tortured, and murdered other human beings in the name of their private interpretations of God or God's Holy Word. O wretched men that we are. Who shall deliver us from this religious quagmire?

God Reigns

God's amazing grace reigns. Out of this history have also come great and marvelous revivals that captured the attention of most of the world and advanced the cause of religion in general and Christianity in particular. So, in spite of ourselves, our God Jehovah maintains a powerful presence in the earth. Despite the confusing and distracting systems men have formed in His name, God reigns.

My point for pointing out ugly religion is to lead us all to rethink how we view our world. I have come to the conclusion that God reigns and is too big to fail, too wise to leave His creation at the mercy of sin-contaminated humankind, and too good to lose His creation to religious confusion and religious bigotry. Furthermore, I contend that human understanding of His ways, means, methods, and mysteries is not a prerequisite for understanding His truth.

Our evangelistic strategy, therefore, should minimize the negative threats and warnings that have traditionally been used to frighten humankind into religious compliance. Instead, our strategy must be to maximize the more positive scenario that wonderfully weaves truth and consequences, complete with mystery and wonder, into the complex tapestry of the everyday human condition. That tapestry includes the good, the bad, and the ugly of our very different journeys. And in that same tight weave, our painful stories are covered by the holy blood of God, which is enough to cover all our shame and allows us all to come home to the eternity that swallows time and its ugly religions, unspeakable human atrocities, tragic natural disasters, countless wars, hate-filled divisions, and even religious sins, mistakes, and miscalculations.

We must dedicate ourselves to overcoming ugly religion, the kind of religion that uses force and fear to dominate, eliminate, and marginalize others. Ugly religion is not certain of its truth to attract, so it substitutes terror. Ugly religion is more about the institution and less about a relationship with the Almighty. Ugly religion is long on theory and human tradition and short on life-giving practice. Ugly religion ignores reality and bases its existence on smoke and mirrors disguised as faith that exploits the pain and suffering of its believers. Ugly religion exercises inhumane authority over the lives of its followers. In ugly religion, mere men have the power of life and death and exercise it before all that others might fear. In ugly religion, the followers worship their human leader and give God honorable mention. In ugly religion, money often replaces ministry, and form is more important than function.

As believers in general and Christian believers in particular, we must lead with the witness of a transcending love that knows no boundaries and can be manifested in the flesh. We must trust Jehovah to bring in those who are of "other folds" without the doubtful disputations that despair of our differences. Our unconditional love must be more radical than our unbending orthodoxies.

Christians must be careful not to fight again the battle Jesus has already won on the cross. The Good News about grace, mercy, and forgiveness must be as freely given as it was received. These qualities must be demonstrated as unlimitedly and unconditionally as is humanly possible, for these graces represent God's goodness, not our own. Their absence makes us unattractive and adds to the confusion.

Nevertheless, the ugliness notwithstanding, I exhort "to all who mourn in Israel, he will give a crown of beauty for ashes, a joyous blessing instead of mourning, festive praise instead of despair. In their righteousness, they will be like great oaks that the LORD has planted for his own glory" (Isaiah 61:3 NLT).

> We now have this light shining in our hearts, but we ourselves are like fragile clay jars containing this great treasure. This makes it clear that our great power is from God, not from ourselves. We are pressed on every side by troubles, but we are not crushed. We are perplexed, but not driven to despair. We are hunted down, but never abandoned by God. We get knocked down, but we are not destroyed.(2 Corinthians 4:7–9 MSG).

The challenges the kingdom of God faces in the world are many, and most are predictable. When we are born into the kingdom of God, we are also born into a war for live territory— the hearts and minds of men and women all over the world. We join a battle between good and evil, God and Satan that will end only when God's purpose is accomplished. Together our mission is to occupy the earth until our God calls an end to life on earth as we know it and calls us home to an eternal reward that, according to God's Word, will be like nothing we have ever imagined.

Until that time, we must endure in faith despite the contradictions and evil eruptions that at times appear stronger than our reason. We must endure the extreme, the radical, and the ugly of our systems of belief, knowing that in the end, the cross of Christ will make the crooked straight and yield beauty for ashes. Our heavenly Father is so good He has done everything possible and necessary to save the world, even though the world has distorted His story.

CHAPTER 13

SO WHAT?

But regarding anything beyond this, dear friend, go easy.
There's no end to the publishing of books, and constant
study wears you out so you're no good for anything else.
The last and final word is this: Fear God. Do what he
tells you.

—ECCLESIASTES 12:13 (MSG)

So what does this all mean? So what if God is as good as has been suggested in this book? Well, from the way most of us were taught and from what I now understand – God's goodness as I understand it today - is a game changer to those who have died in the madness and misery of their sins. It means our minds must change about the mess we've found, the mess we've made, and the mess we will continue to make until the end of all time. It means that all is not lost, that mercy is extended to all who need mercy, not just to those who ask for it. If God is as good as I believe His Word suggests, His plan made in eternity has worked, and at the end of time, He wins back His creation.

So go to sleep with a new confidence that you are saved and safe and cannot easily lose your soul. An overdose of any drug is not greater than God's abundant grace. The nameless, homeless wine-o who dies in the alley and is buried in a pauper's grave is known to his all-wise Father and is covered by the blood of God. God has fixed it—forever.

So what does this all come down to? God's goodness does these seven things:

1. It eliminates the confusion of multiple religions. The mystery must only be endured, not solved. God saves us in spite of our confusion. Just because the creature is confused doesn't mean the Creator is.

2. It levels the playing field. You may have been born into privilege or you may have been born into poverty. However, in eternity you are born again into divine royalty and will kick back at heaven's welcome table with no memory or thought of earthly advantage or disadvantage because of gender, race, age, education, money, height, weight, or religion. You may have been fortunate enough to be born into or have access to a good Bible believing family or church or you may not have had a family or even heard of the church. I tell you with great confidence that the grace and love of your heavenly Father knows you by name and will factor in your personal circumstances.

3. Omnipotence matters. The fact that God wins in the end and carries the whole of creation to victory and creates for us a new heaven and a new earth should be a no-brainer. Of course He wins. He's God. The "gates of hell" DO NOT prevail. He's the Sovereign One who runs this whole thing. He is God, and besides Him there is no other. And according to His Word, nothing in my past and nothing in my future can separate me from His love. Nothing exists that He didn't make. Nothing threatens

Him or His plans. In principle, He gets what He wants. It is the nature of being God. Anything that seems too good to be true is a reflection of the limitation of the creature, not the Creator.

4. It removes the fear of failure. I no longer fear losing my soul. I am not afraid of going to hell. I am not afraid of choosing the wrong religion. I am not afraid of making a mistake or falling into sin.

5. Because of the gifts of His grace and faith, all scripts are rewritten; all sins are negated, erased, and "sent away." I receive a new start as often as I need one.

6. It fulfills the "all that we could ask or think" principle of Ephesians 3:20: "Now all glory to God, who is able, through his mighty power at work within us, to accomplish infinitely more than we might ask or think" (NLT). I have always had a powerful imagination, even from childhood. I have "asked" and imagined that somehow all would be saved, only to find out that God wanted the same thing. I confess, I hedge just slightly when I say, all who *want to* be saved *will* be saved. Nothing is impossible with God.

7. It keeps God's promise of everlasting life for His entire creation and fulfills the desire of God that none should perish except the willing.

Finally, if God is as good as I believe He is, why are we, even in the Christian community, fighting to the death over religious differences? Is it because we believe that Satan somehow still has life even after the death and resurrection of God? Could it be that even we Christians are unsure of the completeness of the victory won at Calvary?

Well, I've got some good news: Jesus won the game for us at Calvary! There will be no rematch. The game has ended. It's over. *Tetelestai* "it is finished!" Jesus died once and for all. He included you and me in His last will and testament. That means my sins are paid and paid forward. When Jesus went to Calvary, I was two thousand years in the future, still in the loins of my ancestral fathers. The acts of sin I was going to commit and the penalty of death that came with them were already paid before I was even born.

The devil committed suicide when he caused the soldier to plunge that spear into Jesus' side, because without the shedding of His precious blood, there would have been no remission for sin. In fact, if the devil had been smart, he would have done everything in his power to keep Jesus alive, because as Adam's disobedience brought death to all humanity, Jesus' death and resurrection brought life to all humanity.

Satan was mortally wounded at Calvary. As prophesied in Genesis 3:15, the seed of the woman crushed his head. We are redeemed from the curse of the law of sin and death. We've won! On the heels of the Calvary victory came the launching of the new offensive, the kingdom of God. It was launched on the day of Pentecost when Jesus sent His replacement, the Holy Spirit, to establish and empower the kingdom and to begin to take dominion and occupy until His triumphant return. So everybody just calm down—this thing was won at Calvary! At Calvary Jesus shouted, "It is finished", threw the mike down and walked off the stage.

CHAPTER 14

A WORD TO THE CHRISTIAN CHURCH

And I say also unto thee, That thou art Peter, and upon this rock I will build my church; and the gates of hell shall not prevail against it. And I will give unto thee the keys of the kingdom of heaven: and whatsoever thou shalt bind on earth shall be bound in heaven: and whatsoever thou shalt loose on earth shall be loosed in heaven.

—MATTHEW 16:18–19 (KJV)

A Word of Balance

God has entrusted believers with great authority—indeed with the very keys of the kingdom of God on earth. These keys were not given to us so we could create kingdoms unto ourselves. The original language of Matthew 16:19 says, "Whatsoever thou shalt bind on earth shall have *already been bound* in heaven; and whatsoever thou shalt loose on earth shall have *already been loosed* in heaven." The point is, everything pertaining to the salvation and restoration of humankind has already been arranged. As the

Christian church, we are His ambassadors only and must keep God's order and instructions as accurately as humanly possible, knowing that our best efforts cannot improve on that order and instruction, but can and probably will diminish it over time.

Again I must say, I believe I understand the fear inherent in hearing perspectives and interpretations that sound too good to be true. But I am also weary of perspectives and interpretations that are too negative and fearful to be true of God. Second Timothy 1:7 reminds us, "God has not given us a spirit of fear, but of power and of love and of a sound mind" (NKJV). I am, consequently, an advocate of balance and reason. I believe God is ultimately and absolutely fair, just, and good. I also believe humanity is imperfect in every way; therefore, I do not believe that the corrupted-by-sin human nature is reliably fair, just, or good.

While I respect and even enjoy human scholarship and opinion, I do not in any absolute or ultimate sense rely on it. I absolutely believe that anyone who hungers and thirsts after righteousness will be satisfied in his spirit by the Holy Spirit of God. Furthermore, I refuse to judge any individual's level of hunger or thirst. I believe God judges "want to," not behavior, and only He can judge that. I am, therefore, delivered from the fear of choosing between scholars or basing my love of God solely on human theology.

The only time Jesus called anyone a viper was when He was referring to the religious leaders of His time, the interpreters of Hebraic law. Times have not changed that much. We still preach our prejudices, practice our perspectives, and demand that the traditions of our upbringing be followed. Some believe to the extreme of bearing arms and killing others who do not believe as they do; while others blacklist those they disagree with and assassinate their characters and reputation in the name of Jesus as proud self-appointed judges of truth and error. Some believe that the Father favors some of His children, but not all. We must, therefore, deliberately and consciously seek balance, and we must beware of the extremes of doubtful disputations.

For the Christian church to strike a balance of perspective as it relates to God and the salvation of His creation, it must first begin with an individual admission and confession of fallibility. After all, Isaiah 64:6 makes it clear: "But we are all as an unclean thing, and all our righteousness are as filthy rags; and we all do fade as a leaf; and our iniquities, like the wind, have taken us away" (KJV). When we acknowledge our own fallibility, it is a small step toward also acknowledging the fallibility of our human institutions, including our religious institutions.

The Roman Catholic Church has for centuries claimed the infallibility of its pope and his right as the apostolic head of Christianity to define ex-cathedra laws and doctrine for all Christians. This claim continued to be made even in the face of historical atrocities, documented crimes, and glaring theological contradictions. Then, in 1517, Martin Luther nailed his Ninety-five Theses to the gate of the Wittenberg cathedral, thus initiating the Protestant Reformation and forever changing the face of Christianity. Interestingly, the Protestant Reformation was not the last reformation. Many of us pledge allegiance today to church organizations that began as reformations of the reformation that preceded it.

Throughout Christianity, the accumulation of tragic human failure by popes, cardinals, bishops, priests, and pastors, which sadly continues to this very day, has sobered the thoughtful and leads to my own plea for balance, inclusion, and the broadening of theological perspective. Keep in mind, not one of us, no matter our position in our chosen religious faith or denomination, will be consulted about who goes to heaven or hell.

It is presumptuous of us to think that we can speak for God without at least an asterisk or disclaimer that confesses fallibility and rests all final judgment of the souls of men exclusively with God. Our ecclesiastical indictments, pronouncements, and judgments are worth only as much as the blood we have shed for a single sinner—which likely is none.

The best we can do as instructors and practitioners is to mitigate our theology, terms, and tone and to humbly submit our thoughts for the perusal of other human beings. In that practice, we can be assured of one thing: the righteous judge will add His anointing to that which is right and cause our human words to become His own.

A Word of Caution

I caution all of us who claim to be servants of the gospel to rethink our presentation, to be revived in the broad hope of God's eternal purpose, to be careful that in our zeal to keep the church clean and heaven holy, we do not misrepresent either God's holiness or His grace.

It is imperative that the Christian churches not re-litigate the gospel of the New Testament, turning it into a book of laws like the Old Testament and thus nullifying all that Jesus accomplished on the cross. The apostle James said if we live by the law, we will die by the law. The glory of the new covenant story is that though the law is holy, just, and good, grace triumphs over law. Yes, we are men and women of sin, but Jesus is our righteousness, and that balances the equation.

The world at its worst needs the church at its best. It is time for some spiritual insurgency. The church must return to its message of spiritual transformation and its demonstration of Spirit and power. We are too given to religious fads and trends, especially those that subtly put us at the center. In 1979, the Spirit of God spoke to me, saying we had stopped using music to worship God and were now using God to worship music. The worship of worship has distracted the church from the work of ministry and inadvertently made common the sacred. As light, we must find darkness and shine in its midst. Many have grown weary of self-serving pomp and circumstance and non-relational, irrelevant religion. May God send revival of His Word and His Holy Spirit, and may we be the peace and unconditional love for which the world hungers.

The greatest threat to the Christian church is irrelevance. If we are to stay in the game and be effective players, we must address the everyday man and woman from the context of our faith. We must focus on what really matters and not be lured into majoring on minors and arguing on the fringes. We must restore credibility to our witness by never advocating something that we cannot practically walk out.

If we are to be relevant, we must respect everybody everywhere, right where they are, and be living proof that what we advocate works indiscriminately, transcending race, gender, nationality, and economic class. Our message must offer the same hope to a Chinese citizen as it does to the schoolteacher in Africa, the cab driver in Israel, the construction worker in the United States, or the farmer in India.

I would caution my Christian friends to stay out of the center of the story. It is not about you, regardless of the size of your church. Be careful about interjecting your unique history and cultural perspective as the standard of behavior for others. Trust God to reveal Himself in ways and means unknown to you. Refuse divisive argument. In Luke 9:49, the disciple John complained to Jesus that someone was casting out devils in Jesus' name, but "he followeth not with us" (KJV). Jesus' answer is instructional: "Forbid him not: for he that is not against us is for us" (KJV). The principle is clear: the kingdom of God is inclusive. The spirit of exclusion, competition, and meanness has no place in God's strategy to save.

> And when his disciples James and John saw this, they said, Lord, wilt thou that we command fire to come down from heaven, and consume them, even as Elias did? But he turned, and rebuked them, and said, Ye know not what manner of spirit ye are of. For the Son of man is not come to destroy men's lives, but to save them.
>
> —LUKE 9:54–56 (KJV)

The spirit and attitude of the church is key to its evangelistic strategy. Those whom we seek to win cannot also be the enemy. If you never mention your Lord's name, share His love because that is who He is and what He is. Remember, you don't have or need all the answers, and you don't have to win.

A Word of Encouragement

My wife often tests the effectiveness of my preaching and especially my counseling by asking me, "How did you leave them? Did you leave them encouraged?" After being raised in a very conservative denomination and starting out as a fire-and-brimstone preacher, I have been matured by the extension of love, grace, and mercy in my own life. Though it took me some time to get there, I am unwilling to claim to know it all in the face of the sovereign will and power of God. I have relaxed as I have encountered His patience and abundant grace. I have been made confident in my personal relationship with the Father and the church's mission in the world:

> All this is from God, who reconciled us to himself
> through Christ and gave us the ministry of
> reconciliation: that God was reconciling the world
> to himself in Christ, not counting men's sins against
> them. And he has committed to us the ministry of
> reconciliation.
>
> —2 Corinthians 5:18–19 (NIV)

God has called and equipped the church to witness, not to win. The fix is in! Jesus won it at Calvary, and no matter how bad things look or may become, God's Word says, "Upon this rock I will build my church; and the gates of hell shall not prevail against it" (Matt. 16:18 KJV). My prayer for the church is reflected in the words of Reinhold Niebuhr's "Serenity Prayer":

> God, grant me the serenity to accept
> The things I cannot change,
> The courage to change the things I can,
> And the wisdom to know the difference.
>
> Living one day at a time,
> Enjoying one moment at a time,
> Accepting hardships as the pathway to peace,
> Taking, as He did,
> This sinful world as it is,
> Not as I would have it,
> Trusting that He will make all things right
> If I surrender to His will,
> That I may be reasonably happy in this life
> And supremely happy with Him forever in the next.
> Amen.

CHAPTER 15

THE BEST NEWS YOU HAVE EVER HEARD IN YOUR LIFE

For God so loved the world, that he gave his only begotten Son, that whosoever believeth in him should not perish, but have everlasting life. For God sent not his Son into the world to condemn the world; but that the world through him might be saved.

—JOHN 3:16–17 (KJV)

Everything I have said up to this final chapter comes full circle in this great passage of Scripture in John 3:16–17. We are not talking about your daddy or your mama or your best friend so loving the world. The passage says *God* so loved the world. For me, that says everything I need to know about God's intentions for you and me. Then, when I keep reading and learn that the plan for my life was made in eternity (Ephesians 1:4), that eternity was my original home and that God, my heavenly Father, has mapped out my purpose and destiny (Psalm 139:16) and planned my escape from the disrupting evil of sin and its consequences, I call that the best news I have ever heard in my life.

Let me explain it in simple, down-to-earth terms. God is too smart and too strong to lose anything to anybody He created, whether it be to humans or to the evil one called Satan that He created as the tester of humanity. You might believe the devil was once a right-doing angel who went rogue and was defeated and demoted, or you might believe, as I do, that he was intentionally created to be what he has always been and is today. Regardless of your position, the fact remains that evil does not exist on its own. The evil that supposedly seduced Lucifer had an origin, and the Bible is very clear that absolutely nothing exists that God did not create, good or evil.

John 1:3 says, "All things were made by him; and without him was not any thing made that was made" (KJV). Colossians 1:16 says, "For by him were all things created, that are in heaven, and that are in earth, visible and invisible, whether they be thrones, or dominions, or principalities, or powers: all things were created by him, and for him" (KJV). Isaiah 54:16 repeats the same thought: "Behold, I have created the smith that bloweth the coals in the fire, and that bringeth forth an instrument for his work; and I have created the waster to destroy" (KJV). Isaiah 45:7 states, "I form the light, and create darkness; I make peace, and create evil: I the LORD do all these things."

My point? Any way you look at it, the devil is God's devil, and that's great news. Furthermore, God has given us authority over him: "Behold, I give unto you power to tread on serpents and scorpions, and over all the power of the enemy: and nothing shall by any means hurt you" (Luke 10:19 KJV). You see, the point is, God is not a part-time deity. Everything He does is intentional and eternal. So when He chose to create the earth and to give authority and dominion to the humans He created as the crowning glory of it all, it was certain that His will would be accomplished on earth as it is in heaven.

Want to hear some more very good news? God has made it all but impossible to go to hell. If a person goes to hell, he must overcome the most powerful act of love that has ever existed. To go to hell, one must turn a deaf ear to the voice of the soul and a blind eye to the beauty of creation. To go to hell, one must hide his heart from God until it is so hard it can no longer respond. To go to hell, one must work at it. If you do nothing, His love will find you and woo you in a language you understand, whether it is a Bantu dialect or the mysterious tongue of a "stoned out of his mind" alcoholic like my uncle Percy who would pray and weep while drunk with wine. Having already redeemed you by His blood sacrifice on the cross, He will seduce you into wanting Him. He will forgive you, love you, win you and reveal your purpose to you. He has sent me to tell you to come on home; He is not mad at you. Your big brother Jesus has paid your penalty (2 Corintians 5:16–21). And He is ready to help you live a new lifestyle that will maximize your purpose on earth.

The news gets even better. All the prodigal son of Luke 15:11–32 had to do was to want out of the pigpen. He didn't know his daddy had already forgiven him and was waiting for any sign of his return home. The prodigal son's repentance was for him, not for his father. The father never heard his son's words of remorse or responded to his words of repentance. Could it be that the father had already made the decision? "Welcome home, son. Whew! You scared me for a minute. I thought I had lost you. Dang, boy! You look a mess, and you stink like a pig. Well, a little soap and water and you'll be fine. Here, put this ring on. Hey, everybody, my baby boy is home. Here, son, when you come out of the shower, put this robe on. Somebody put some steaks on the grill. One of y'all go to the corner store and bring a case of their best… whatever. And invite the neighborhood over. They saw him leave, now see him come back home. It's party time!"

The wonder is that God in his fathomless omnipotence and omniscience would condescend to use a creature He made out of dirt and imprint on this dirt-creature His Holy image; that we mere humans are endowed by the Creator with His supernatural anointing wrapped around a carnal, earthly, limited vessel that He knows will fall, fail, and flounder - often; yet, He calls and causes them to be Holy as He is… then as an Infinite Sovereign - arbitrarily declares it to be so. And finally, what is more, covered by His Holy and Righteous blood, the worse and the best of us will go sweeping through the gates of paradise.

Could God be this good? If not, then why am I weeping? I rest my case with the remainder of the song I started in chapter one entitled "The Love Of God":

> The love of God is greater far
> Than tongue or pen can ever tell;
> It goes beyond the highest star,
> And reaches to the lowest hell;
> The guilty pair, bowed down with care,
> God gave His Son to win;
> His erring child He reconciled,
> And pardoned from his sin.
>
> When years of time shall pass away,
> And earthly thrones and kingdoms fall,
> When men, who here refuse to pray,
> On rocks and hills and mountains call;
> God's love so sure, shall still endure,
> All measureless and strong;
> Redeeming grace to Adam's race—
> The saints' and angels' song.
>
> Could we with ink the ocean fill,
> And were the skies of parchment made,

Were every stalk on earth a quill,
And every man a scribe by trade;
To write the love of God above
Would drain the ocean dry;
Nor could the scroll contain the whole,
Though stretched from sky to sky.

Chorus:
O love of God, how rich and pure!
How measureless and strong! It shall forevermore
endure—
The saints' and angels' song.

Could God be this good? Yes, God is this good!

Author's Contact Information:

Dr. M. Tyrone Cushman Sr.
Website: www.tyronecushman.com
E-mail: tyronecushman@gmail.com
Cell Phone: (210) 602-3894

Or

Carmen M. Cushman, Administrator
(210) 309-7252

Other Books by This Author

God of Our Weary Years
(The Reconciliation of Race and Faith)

About the Author

M ichael Tyrone Cushman Sr. was born and raised in the 8 Mile Rd. projects of Detroit, Michigan. He holds a Bachelor of Arts degree with majors in Sociology and History from Wayne State University. He received the Honorary Doctor of Divinity from the Southern California School of Ministry where he taught Old Testament Survey and Bible Doctrine. He has pastored for 41 years including 5 years as General Overseer of the National Association of the Church of God. He and his childhood sweetheart Jackie were married 45 years before she passed away August 12, 2013. He is founder and Bishop of United Ministries International overseeing Senior Pastors in the U. S. and Kenya East Africa.

Dr. Cushman is a much sought after preacher, teacher and lecturer and can be contacted for teaching and preaching engagements at:

Ms. Carmen Cushman, Administrator
(210) 309-7252
Dr. M. Tyrone Cushman
(210) 602-3498
tyronecushman@gmail.com